Sir Arthur Conan Doyle

The Sign of Four

Retold by **Nancy Timmins**

Activities by **Eleanor Donaldson**

Illustrated by **Massimo Valenti**

Editor: Rebecca Raynes
Design and art direction: Nadia Maestri
Computer graphics: Simona Corniola
Picture research: Laura Lagomarsino

© 2007   Black Cat

First edition: April 2007

Picture credits
By courtesy of the National Portrait Gallery, London: 4,
83; The Granger Collection, New York: 6; © Michael
Jenner / Alamy: 18; By permission of the British Library:
85; © Thierry Falise / Onasia.com: 109; © LOOK Die
Bildagentur der Fotografen GmbH / Alamy: 111.

We would be happy to receive your comments and
suggestions, and give you any other information
concerning our material.

www.blackcat-cideb.com

ISBN 978-88-530-0597-7   Book + CD

Printed in Italy by Litoprint, Genoa

Contents

This story is recorded in full.

These symbols indicate the beginning and end of the passages
linked to the listening activities.

Sir Arthur Conan Doyle (1927) by Henry L. Gates.

Sir Arthur Conan Doyle

Sir Arthur Conan Doyle was born in Edinburgh in 1859 and died in 1930. During his life he had many different interests and was talented in many of them. He studied medicine at Edinburgh University, where he worked with the surgeon Professor Joseph Bell. It is thought that Conan Doyle used Professor Bell and his use of the science of deduction as a model for the character of Sherlock Holmes.

Conan Doyle began his career as a doctor in Southsea and it was while he was waiting for patients that he began to write. His success as an author allowed him to stop working as a doctor and turn his attention to other subjects. He is best known for his creation of Sherlock Holmes and Doctor Watson. The two characters first appeared in *A Study In Scarlet* which was published in *Beeton's Christmas Annual* in 1887. In 1890, the second Sherlock Holmes novel, *The Sign of Four*, was published: it firmly established Holmes and Watson in literary history.

Conan Doyle wrote other novels which were more serious in content than the Sherlock Holmes stories, but they were less popular. Historical novels such as *Micah Clarke* (1888), *Rodney Stone* (1896) and *The Exploits of Brigadier Gerard* (1903) were successful at the time of publishing but are little known today.

The Holmes stories were so popular that Conan Doyle felt that the character was almost too successful. In 1893, he published a novel called *The Adventure of the Final Problem,* in which Sherlock Holmes was killed. But the public demanded that Sherlock Holmes was brought back to life: Conan Doyle responded by writing *The Hound of the Baskervilles* (1902). He wrote the novel as if it had happened before the time of Sherlock Holmes' death.

However, in one of his later novels, *The Lost World* (1912), Conan Doyle turned to science fiction and again created a character that caught the imagination of readers both then and now; Professor Challenger. *The Lost World* was first released as a silent film in 1925, and again in 1960. Stephen Spielberg made a film called *The Lost World* in 1997 but it was not based on Conan Doyle's novel, although it is about dinosaurs. It is a sequel to *Jurassic Park* which was based on the novel by the modern writer Michael Crichton.

Politics was one of Conan Doyle's interests in later life and some of the characters in *The Lost World* were thought to be based on political figures of the time. He campaigned to prove the innocence of individuals and helped to introduce the Court of Criminal Appeal. Other interests in his life included spiritualism and trying to prove the existence of fairies. This seems strange given that in the earlier part of his life he was so interested in logic and reason, but it can perhaps be explained by the loss of both his father and his wife in a short space of time.

The photograph of Frances Griffiths and the fairies made by her cousin with paper cutouts, which Conan Doyle believed was real.

He was given the title 'Sir' for his work as a doctor in the Boer War. The French named Conan Doyle 'The Good Giant'. This seems appropriate as his many various achievements always seemed to be working towards the general good of humanity.

1 Comprehension check
Answer these questions.

1 Who did Arthur Conan Doyle use as a model for Sherlock Holmes?
2 What was Arthur Conan Doyle's early career?
3 Name three of his detective novels.
4 Name two other novels he wrote.
5 What other interests did he have?
6 What name did the French give him?

2 Summary
Put these sentences in order to make a summary of Sir Arthur Conan Doyle's life and career as they appear in the text.

A ☐ He 'killed' Sherlock Holmes in *The Final Problem*.
B ☐ He wrote his first Sherlock Holmes book.
C ☐ He invented the character of Professor Challenger.
D ☐ He was given the title of 'Sir'.
E ☐ He began to work as a doctor in Southsea.
F ☐ He studied medicine at Edinburgh University.
G ☐ He wrote *The Sign of Four*.
H ☐ He lost his wife and father.

The Characters

Back row: Jonathan Small, Thaddeus Sholto, Major Sholto, Bartholomew Sholto, Athelney Jones
Front row: Tonga, Watson, Holmes, Miss Morstan

Before you read

2 **1** **Listening**

FCE

Listen to the first part of Chapter One and tick (✓) A, B or C.

1 Why is Holmes bored?
   A ☐ He hasn't got a case to work on.
   B ☐ He's the only unofficial detective.
   C ☐ He's relaxing after lunch.

2 Holmes gives advice to other detectives because
   A ☐ they don't know what to do.
   B ☐ the work gives him pleasure.
   C ☐ they don't want an expert opinion.

3 Watson wrote a book called
   A ☐ *The Jefferson Hope Case.*
   B ☐ *A Study in Scarlet.*
   C ☐ *The Power of Observation and Deduction.*

4 Holmes knows that Watson went to the post office because
   A ☐ Watson came home with a letter.
   B ☐ Watson needed some stamps and envelopes.
   C ☐ his shoes are dirty.

5 Holmes deduces that Watson went to the post office to
   A ☐ send a letter.
   B ☐ send a telegram.
   C ☐ buy some stamps.

6 Watson then asks Holmes to deduce something about the previous owner of
   A ☐ the house.
   B ☐ his book.
   C ☐ his watch.

CHAPTER **ONE**

The Science of Deduction

It was afternoon. Holmes and I were sitting in our living room in 221B Baker Street, relaxing after our lunch.

'I hate to be bored,' said Holmes suddenly. I looked over at him.

'Are you bored now?' I asked. I myself was feeling rather content.

'Yes,' he replied. 'I need something to occupy my mind. That's why I have chosen my particular profession, or rather, created it, as I'm the only one in the world.'

'The only unofficial detective?' I asked.

'The only unofficial consulting detective,'[1] he corrected me. 'When Gregson or Lestrade or Athelney Jones don't know what to do — which they normally don't — then they come to me. I give them an expert opinion. I take no credit for it. It's the work itself which gives me pleasure. But there is no work at the moment, so I am bored.'

---

1. **consulting detective** : a detective that people go to for help.

I had some experience of Holmes' work in the Jefferson Hope case. I had written a small book about the case, calling it 'A Study in Scarlet'. Sherlock Holmes did not like it. He said it was too romantic. 'My name has also extended to the continent,' continued Holmes. 'I was consulted last week by a French detective. He had two out of the three qualities necessary for a good detective. He has the power of observation and of deduction. He doesn't have knowledge, but that will come with experience.

'But aren't observation and deduction the same thing?' I asked.

'Oh no,' he answered. 'For example, observation tells me that you have been to the Wigmore Street Post Office this morning, but deduction tells me that when you were there, you sent a telegram.'

'You're right!' I exclaimed. 'But how did you know?'

'It's quite simple,' he laughed. 'I can observe that you have some red coloured earth on your shoe. That's observation. Just opposite the Wigmore Street Post Office they are digging up the road. The earth they have dug up is the same colour, which can't be found anywhere else in the area. That is deduction.'

'And what about the telegram?'

'I knew you hadn't written a letter because I was with you all morning. I also saw that you already have stamps and envelopes. So that only leaves one reason to go to the post office: to send a telegram.'

'How simple!' I replied. 'Can you put your skills to a more difficult test?'

'Of course,' said Holmes. 'What is it?'

I gave him a watch that I had had for only a short time.

'What can you tell me about the character or habits of the

late [1] owner of this watch?' I asked. Secretly I wanted him to get it wrong. Sometimes his know-it-all tone became annoying.

He looked at the watch for some time, opening the back and examining it carefully. He handed it back to me.

'It has recently been cleaned,' he said, 'which has taken away many clues.' [2]

'You're right,' I said. I did not think this was a very good excuse.

'But I can say,' he continued, 'that this watch belonged to your elder brother, who inherited it from your father.'

'Ah, the initials H.W. on the back. Right so far. Anything else?' I asked.

'Your brother was an untidy man and very careless. He was poor for a lot of the time with occasional times when he had money. He finally began drinking heavily and he died. That's all I can tell.'

I felt disappointed and angry. How could he tell all that from a watch? It was all true, but I was sure that he had found out about my poor unhappy brother from other people.

'You're very unkind!' I said to him. 'Don't pretend to deduce what you have been told by others!'

'Dear Doctor Watson, I'm sorry!' he said. 'I forgot how personal and upsetting it might be to you. But I promise that I didn't even know you had a brother until you gave me that watch.'

'Then how did you know these facts? You were right about everything.'

Holmes told me. 'In England, when pawnbrokers [3] take a

---

1. **late** : recently dead.
2. **clues** : clues to a problem or mystery help you to find the answer to it.
3. **pawnbrokers** : people who lend money in return for a valuable item (e.g. a watch), which can be sold if the money is not paid back in time.

watch, they scratch [1] the number of the ticket on the watch with a pin. I noticed that there were four small numbers scratched onto the back of the watch. This means that your brother often didn't have much money, so he took the watch to a pawnbrokers four times, but then he also often had enough money to buy it back. Also if you look at where you wind up the watch, [2] you'll see many little scratches. This is where the key for winding it up has slipped. [3] It slipped because he was often drunk when he went to bed and was trying to wind up his watch.'

There was a knock at the door.

'There's a young lady to see you, sir,' said our landlady. [4] 'A Miss Mary Morstan.'

'Hmm,' said Holmes, 'I don't know the name. Show her in. You stay as well, Doctor.'

Miss Morstan entered the room. She was a young attractive lady with blonde hair and large blue eyes. She seemed agitated.

'I've come to ask for your help, Mr Holmes,' she said, 'because you once helped my employer, Mrs Cecil Forrester, with a small problem. She recommended you.'

'Yes, I think I remember,' said Holmes. 'A very simple case.'

'She didn't think so. But you can't say the same about my case. Let me tell you about my strange situation.'

Sherlock Holmes looked excited. 'Tell me all about it,' he said.

---

1. **scratch** : make small thin cuts on the surface.
2. **wind up the watch** : turn a small key or device on it several times in order to make it operate.
3. **slipped** : accidentally moved out of place.
4. **landlady** : lady who owns their flat but allows them to live in it in return for money.

The text and **beyond**

1 Comprehension check

Decide if these sentences about Chapter One are true (T) or false (F). Correct the false ones.

		T	F
1	Holmes is the only unofficial consulting detective in the world.	☐	☐
2	Doctor Watson had written a small book about a French detective.	☐	☐
3	Holmes criticises Watson's writing.	☐	☐
4	Observation and deduction are the same.	☐	☐
5	Holmes observed that Watson went to the post office that morning.	☐	☐
6	Watson could guess what Holmes had done that day by using simple clues.	☐	☐
7	Watson asked Holmes to guess the original owner of his watch.	☐	☐
8	The watch belonged to his friend who lived in London.	☐	☐
9	Watson was upset when Holmes deduced correctly.	☐	☐
10	The watch was taken to a pawnbroker four times.	☐	☐
11	The lady who came to visit them was very attractive.	☐	☐
12	She came to see Holmes because he once helped her sister.	☐	☐

2 Characters

Which of these sentences are about Watson? Which are about Holmes? Tick (✓) the correct box.

		W	H
1	He is the only unofficial consulting detective in the world.	☐	☐
2	He believes in logical explanations.	☐	☐
3	He has a romantic idea of detective work.	☐	☐

4   He has the title of 'Doctor'. ☐ ☐

5   He is easily bored. ☐ ☐

6   His brother did not have an easy life. ☐ ☐

7   He is easily surprised. ☐ ☐

8   He is confident of his abilities. ☐ ☐

9   He notices very small details. ☐ ☐

10 He is rather critical. ☐ ☐

3 Observations and deductions

Read these 'observations'. Match them to the 'deductions'.

1 ☐ A man has mud on his shoes and some black and white hair on his trousers.

2 ☐ A woman goes through security and does not check in at an airport.

3 ☐ A well-dressed man is sleeping on a bench in a small station.

4 ☐ A wealthy man asks where he can find a phone box. He has a mobile phone.

5 ☐ A 20-year-old woman arrives with some other women to pick up two children aged 10 and 12.

6 ☐ The man is the last person to leave a bar. He is not drunk, but he is tired.

A He had missed the last train and there were no taxis.

B He works there. He has just closed it.

C She is the babysitter.

D She works as an air-hostess.

E He was taking his dog for a walk.

F The battery of his mobile phone was dead and he had to make an urgent call.

4 **Deductions**

Observe the picture of Sherlock Holmes' room. What can you deduce about Sherlock Holmes?

Example: He smokes a pipe.

5 **Listening**

You will hear a conversation between a woman and a pawnbroker. For each sentence decide which object they are talking about.

A the gold bracelet   **B** the pearl necklace   **C** the diamond ring

1. ☐ It is pretty but they are probably false.
2. ☐ The woman receives 5 pounds for it.
3. ☐ Her husband gave it to her.
4. ☐ It belonged to her grandmother.
5. ☐ The pawnbroker still has it.
6. ☐ The woman's son found it.

6 Speaking

Which of the things in the picture do you use to communicate with? Tell another student which type of communication you like best, and why.

Example: I like writing emails because I can write more than a text message.

7 Writing

Read Watson's telegram below. Rewrite the message in simple, modern English as a text message. (Remember you do not need the person's name and you can use simple abbreviations if you know them).

Example: How RU? Thx...

> Anne STOP thank you for the return of the watch STOP the cheque is in the post STOP I hope you are well STOP Until I have the pleasure of your next visit STOP Watson

Before you read

① Listening

FCE

Listen to the beginning of Chapter Two. For questions 1-6, choose the best answer — A, B or C.

1   What was Miss Morstan's father's job?
   A   ☐   He was the the captain of a ship.
   B   ☐   He was in the army.
   C   ☐   He was a teacher at a school.

2   What happened to her father?
   A   ☐   He died.
   B   ☐   He joined the police.
   C   ☐   He disappeared.

3   Did her father know anyone in London?
   A   ☐   He knew a man from the same regiment.
   B   ☐   He knew a Major, but he was not in England.
   C   ☐   He knew no one in England anymore.

4   What did she see in *The Times* newspaper?
   A   ☐   an article about her
   B   ☐   an important address
   C   ☐   an advertisement

5   What had she received once a year for the last six years?
   A   ☐   a large box
   B   ☐   a small pearl
   C   ☐   a large pearl

6   What did she give to Holmes?
   A   ☐   a letter
   B   ☐   a pearl
   C   ☐   a box

CHAPTER **TWO**

A New Case

I got up to leave but the young lady stopped me.

'You may also be able to help me,' she said. I sat down again.

'These are the facts,' she continued. 'My father was an officer in an Indian regiment. My mother was dead, so I went to boarding school [1] in Edinburgh until I was seventeen. In the year 1878, my father had a year's leave [2] from the military and he came home. He wrote to me and told me to meet him in London at the Langham Hotel. When I arrived, they told me that he was staying there but had gone out the night before and hadn't returned. I waited all day but there was no news. Eventually I contacted the police. But from that day to this, nothing has been heard of my father.'

The poor girl was trying not to cry.

'What was the date?' asked Holmes.

---

1. **boarding school** : a school where the pupils live and sleep as well as being educated.
2. **leave** : time off (usually from the military or other armed forces).

'He disappeared on the third of December, 1878, nearly ten years ago.'

'Did he have any bags?'

'Yes, but there was nothing in them that gave any clue about what had happened. Clothes, books, some things from the Andaman Islands.[1] That was where he was based,' she explained.

'Did he have any friends in town?' asked Holmes.

'Only one,' she replied, 'Major Sholto, who was in the same regiment as my father. He was retired and lived in Upper Norwood.[2] He didn't even know that my father was in England.'

She continued. 'About six years ago, on the fourth of May, 1882, I saw an advertisement in *The Times* newspaper, asking for the address of Miss Mary Morstan. It said that she would receive good news if she communicated her address. So, I put it in the newspaper. The next day, a small box was brought to my house. Inside there was a very large and beautiful pearl. There was nothing else, no message, no address, nothing. Since then, on the same date every year, another box has arrived, each containing another pearl.'

She opened a small box as she was speaking. Inside were six beautiful pearls.

'Most interesting,' said Holmes. 'Has anything else happened?'

'Yes, today. That's why I've come to see you. This morning I received this letter.' She gave the letter to Holmes for him to read.

'"Be outside the Lyceum Theatre tonight at seven o'clock,"' he read. '"If you feel safer, bring two friends. You deserve justice

1. **Andaman Islands** : a group of two hundred islands in the Bay of Bengal, India.
2. **Upper Norwood** : area in South London.

and you shall have it. Do not bring the police. Your unknown friend." Well, what a mystery! And what do you want to do, Miss Morstan?' he asked.

'That's why I'm here,' she said.

'We will go then — you and I and — yes, Doctor Watson can come too. We have worked together before.'

Miss Morstan looked at me. 'Will you come, doctor?' she asked.

'I'll be happy to,' I replied.

'You're both very kind,' she said. 'I'll be here at six then.'

'One last thing,' said Holmes. 'The handwriting in the letter; is it the same as that on the pearl boxes?'

'I have them here,' she said, giving them to Holmes.

He spread them out on the table and compared them.

'Yes,' he said after a moment. 'The writer has tried to change his handwriting each time, but they are definitely written by the same person. Is this handwriting anything like your father's, Miss Morstan?'

'Not at all,' she said.

'I thought so,' said Holmes. 'We'll see you at six then.'

Miss Morstan left the room.

I looked out of the window and watched her walking away.

'What an attractive woman,' I exclaimed, turning to Holmes.

'Is she?' he said. 'I didn't notice.' Holmes got up. 'I'm going out,' he said. 'There are a few things I want to find out.'

I sat at the window. I could not stop thinking about Miss Mary Morstan: her smile, the sound of her voice, and the mystery that was part of her life. 'If she was seventeen when her father disappeared, that must make her twenty-seven now,' I thought, 'a nice age.' I sat thinking about her until my thoughts became dangerous: who was I to hope for such things? A retired and injured army surgeon with little money — no, it was better to forget such thoughts of happiness with Miss Morstan.

Holmes returned at half past five. He seemed very happy.

'This isn't such a great mystery,' he said. 'There seems to be only one explanation.'

'What! You've solved it already?' I asked.

'Oh no,' he said. 'But I have discovered an important fact. I've been looking at old copies of *The Times* and I've found out that Major Sholto died on the twenty-eighth of April, 1882.'

'And so? I'm sorry, I don't understand, Holmes.'

'No? You do surprise me. Look at it this way. Captain Morstan disappears. The only person he knows in London is Major Sholto. Major Sholto says he didn't know Morstan was in London. Four years later, Major Sholto dies. Only a week after his death, Captain Morstan's daughter receives a valuable present, which is repeated every year. Now she gets a letter which says that she deserves justice. What else can it mean except justice for the loss of her father? Why did the presents begin immediately after Sholto's death? It must mean that Sholto's heir [1] knows something about the mystery and wants to compensate Mary Morstan.'

'But how strange! Why has he written now, and not six years ago? And anyway, what justice can she have? You don't really think her father is still alive do you? What other injustice is there in her case?'

Sherlock Holmes thought for a moment. 'It's true, Watson,

---

1. **heir** : someone who has the right to inherit a person's property or money when that person dies.

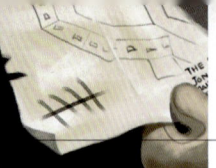

there are problems. But I think our journey tonight will solve them all. Are you ready? I think Miss Morstan is downstairs in a cab.'[1]

I picked up my hat and my stick. Holmes took a gun from a drawer and put it in his pocket. It seemed that things might get serious.

In the cab, Sherlock Holmes asked Miss Morstan some more questions.

'Major Sholto was a very good friend of Papa's,' she said. 'He and Papa were in charge of the soldiers on the Andaman Islands. They spent a lot of time together. By the way,' she continued, 'a strange paper was found in Papa's desk. No one can understand it, but I brought it to show you. Here it is.'

Holmes studied the paper carefully.

'It was made in India,' he said. 'It is a plan of a large building with many rooms and passages. In one place there is a small cross in red ink and above it is written, "3.37 from left". In the left-hand corner is a strange hieroglyph[2] like four crosses in a line with their arms touching. Beside it is written "The sign of the four — Jonathan Small, Mahomet Singh, Abdullah Khan, Dost Akbar".

'No, I don't know what this is about. But it is obviously an important document because it has been kept very carefully. It is very clean.'

Holmes leaned back. He was thinking hard.

1. **cab** : taxi; here, carriage with horses.
2. **hieroglyph** : a form of writing using picture symbols, especially used in ancient Egypt.

THE SIGN OF THE FOUR
JONATHAN SMALL
MAHOMET SINGH
ABDULLAH KHAN
DOST AKBAR

The text and **beyond**

FCE ❶ **Comprehension check**

For questions 1-6 choose the answer — A, B, C or D — which you think fits best according to the text.

1 When did the girl's father disappear?
A ☐ When he was in India.
B ☐ When she was at boarding school.
C ☐ One night when he was staying in a London hotel.
D ☐ Ten years after he arrived home.

2 What did her father have with him?
A ☐ Some clothes from the Andaman Islands.
B ☐ Some clothes, books and other things from abroad.
C ☐ Some books and a bag.
D ☐ Some books from the Andaman Islands in a bag.

3 What arrived one day for Miss Morstan?
A ☐ A small pearl in a large box.
B ☐ A very large pearl in a small box.
C ☐ A large pearl in a piece of newspaper.
D ☐ A pearl necklace in a small box.

4 What did Miss Morstan's letter say?
A ☐ 'You deserve justice.'
B ☐ 'We must meet inside the theatre.'
C ☐ 'Do not bring anyone.'
D ☐ 'I am your friend.'

5 What did Dr Watson think of Miss Morstan?
A ☐ He thought her story was interesting.
B ☐ He thought she looked older than her real age.
C ☐ He thought she was mysterious.
D ☐ He thought she was very attractive.

6 Who is trying to compensate Mary Morstan?
A ☐ Sherlock Holmes
B ☐ Captain Morstan
C ☐ Major Sholto's heir
D ☐ Doctor Watson

2 Dates and events

Match the dates (A-C) to the events below. There can be more than one answer for each date.

A 1878 **B** 1882 **C** 1888

1. ☐ Captain Morstan returned to London.
2. ☐ Miss Morstan received a letter from a stranger.
3. ☐ Major Sholto died.
4. ☐ Captain Morstan disappeared.
5. ☐ An advertisement in *The Times* asked for Mary Morstan's address.
6. ☐ Miss Morstan recieved the first pearl.

3 Vocabulary

Major Sholto was in the army. Sherlock Holmes helps the police. Look at the words in the box and decide whether they are connected to the army or the police. Add any other words you know connected to the work of the police or the army. Use a dictionary if necessary.

Scotland Yard inspector detective captain soldier
major Navy Marines constable police station

Army	Police

4 Speaking

Discuss these questions with another student.

1   Doctor Watson worked as an army surgeon. What other jobs can you do in the army other than be a soldier?

2   Do the police and the army in your country sometimes do the same type of work?

5 Advertisement

Read the advertisement from *The Times.* Find the mistakes. Rewrite the message so that it reads in the way Miss Morstan described.

Looking for: Captain Morstan

This person should send a telegram immediately with a home address to Mr Sholto.

We have something valuable. The gentleman will receive good news if he replies.

 ## 6 Writing

Last month you made a new friend. Another friend, Jim, wants to know about him/her. Write a letter to Jim explaining how you met, what things you have in common, what you particularly like about him or her and your plans, if any, to meet again.
Write your letter in 120-180 words.

Before you read

1 Reading pictures

Look at the picture on pages 32-33. Answer these questions.

1   Describe the room.

2   Describe the man.

3   Who do you think lives in this house?

4   Why are Sherlock Holmes, Watson and Miss Morstan here?

CHAPTER **THREE**

The Story of the Bald-Headed Man

We arrived at the Lyceum Theatre. There were already a lot of **people outside. We got out of the cab and a small man came up to us.**

'Are you with Miss Morstan?' he asked us.

'I'm Miss Morstan, and these two gentlemen are my friends,' she said.

'Can you promise that neither of your friends is a policeman?' he asked.

Miss Morstan promised. The man took us to a cab; we climbed inside and the man drove the cab. We moved away quickly through the streets. At first I knew where we were going, but I was soon lost. Holmes of course knew exactly where we were.

'Priory Road. Robert Street. Cold Harbour Lane. Not very nice areas,' he said. Finally the cab stopped outside a house in a row of other houses. They all looked empty. We knocked at the door and it was opened by an Indian servant.

'He's waiting for you,' he said.

We heard another voice from a room further inside.

'Bring them in,' it said. 'Bring them straight in.'

The servant took us to a door and opened it. In the room was
a small man with a bald head. He had a hanging lower lip which
showed a line of irregular, yellow teeth. Although he was bald he
did not look old; he was in fact thirty years old.

'Come in, come in,' he said. He seemed nervous.

The room was very different to the rest of the house and the area. It was brightly coloured and luxurious, in an Oriental style.

'My name is Thaddeus Sholto,' the man said. 'You are Miss Morstan, and these gentlemen...?'

'Sherlock Holmes and Doctor Watson.'

'So, to begin,' he said. 'Your father, Miss Morstan, is dead.'

She went white, but then said, 'I had hoped he was still alive, but I knew in my heart that he wasn't.'

Thaddeus Sholto continued.

'I can tell you everything, and I can also give you justice, whatever my brother Bartholomew says. We'll have to go to Norwood to see him, but he's very angry with me for doing what I think is right. He can be a terrible person when he's angry.'

'Let's go as soon as possible then; it's already late,' I said.

'First of all, I must tell you what I know,' he said.

'My father was Major John Sholto. He retired eleven years ago and came to live at Pondicherry House in Norwood. He was a rich man and brought Indian servants with him and lived in luxury. My twin brother Bartholomew and I were the only children. I remember when Captain Morstan disappeared. We talked about it often with my father: we never suspected that he knew exactly what happened to Captain Morstan.

'We did know that our father was in some sort of danger, though. He did not go out alone and he was very scared of men with wooden legs. Once, he even fired his gun at a man with a wooden leg, who was just a salesman trying to sell something. We had to pay him a lot of money to keep the matter quiet.

'In 1882, he received a letter from India, which was a great shock to him. He never told us what it said, but from that day he became ill, until the doctor told us he was close to death. He wanted to tell us something before he died.

'When we went in to see him, he looked terrible. He told us to lock the door and come to either side of the bed. This is what he said.

'"I have treated Morstan's daughter terribly. I have been a greedy man; at least half of the treasure belongs to her. See that string of pearls there; that is part of the treasure. I was going to send it to her. You, my sons, I want you to make sure that she gets half of the Agra treasure. But don't send anything until I am dead.

"'I'll tell you how Morstan died," he continued. "For many years, he had a weak heart but only I knew about it. When we were in India, by luck, he and I found a large amount of valuable treasure. I brought it over to England. When Morstan arrived in London, he came to claim his share. [1] We argued about how to divide the treasure between us. We were shouting at each other and he was very angry. Suddenly he put his hand to his side, his face changed colour and he fell backwards, hitting his head on the treasure chest. He was dead.

"'I didn't know what to do. I didn't want to call the police, because it looked like I had killed him, and I didn't want other people to know about the treasure. I was thinking about it when my servant came to the door. 'Don't worry, sir,' he said. 'I won't tell anyone that you killed him. We'll hide the body and nobody will know anything.' I made a decision; if my own servant thought that I killed him, then the police were certainly not going to believe me. So we hid Morstan's body and the treasure. It is only right that Morstan's daughter gets her share. Come closer and I'll tell you where it is. The treasure is hidden in —"

'At this moment, his face changed. He looked scared and he began to shout: 'Keep him out! Keep him out!' We looked around at the window behind us where he was staring. [2] There was a face looking in from the darkness. It was a bearded face with wild cruel eyes and an evil expression. We rushed to the window,

---

1. **claim his share** : try to get his part because he thinks he has a right to it.
2. **staring** : looking for a long time.

but there was no one there. When we returned to our father, his heart had stopped beating.

'We searched the garden that night but all we found was a single foot print below the window. We thought we had imagined it but the next day, the window of my father's room was found open. Someone had searched his room and on his chest was a note with the words "The sign of the four" written on it. We never knew who it was or what it meant. Nothing was stolen.'

He stopped speaking for a moment. Miss Morstan looked white, and she drank the glass of water I gave her. Sherlock Holmes leaned back in his chair. Thaddeus continued his story.

'My brother and I wanted to find the treasure that our father told us about. We searched everywhere, digging in the garden, looking in every part of the house. But we didn't find it. We knew by the quality of the pearls that the treasure was worth a lot of money. My brother is very like my father; he is also very greedy — he didn't want to send the pearls to Miss Morstan. But finally I persuaded him to send a pearl once a year to Miss Morstan so that she had something of value.'

'It was very kind of you,' said Miss Morstan.

'We had to make sure justice was done,' said Thaddeus. 'At least, that's what I thought. Bartholomew didn't agree. That's why I moved out of Pondicherry House.'

'So why are we here now?' asked Holmes.

'Yesterday, I found out that the treasure has been discovered. I contacted Miss Morstan. And now we must go to Norwood and claim our share of it. I told Bartholomew what I wanted to do, so he'll be expecting us, even if he doesn't want to see us.'

'You've done well, sir,' said Holmes. 'Let's go.'

The text and **beyond**

① **Comprehension check**

Complete the questions about Chapter Three with *who,* or *what* and then answer them.

1 .... opened the door to them?

2 .... was the man in the room?

3 .... did Major Sholto's sons often talk about?

4 .... was Major Sholto scared of?

5 .... did Major Sholto receive from India?

6 .... did Major Sholto and Captain Morstan argue about?

7 .... killed Captain Morstan?

8 .... did they see at the window?

9 .... did they find on their father's chest?

10 .... lives in Pondicherry House now?

FCE ② **Summary**

Read this summary of Major Sholto's story. Think of the word that best fits each space. Use only one word for each space. There is an example at the beginning (0).

Before Major Sholto died he (**0**) ..told......... his sons about the treasure and Captain Morstan. This is what he told (**1**) ....

He and Captain Morstan (**2**) .... found a large amount of valuable treasure (**3**) .... India. Major Sholto (**4**) .... it to England. One day he and Captain Morstan argued about how to (**5**) .... the treasure. Captain Morstan had a weak heart. (**6**) .... they were arguing he became very angry. He fell backwards, hit his head on the treasure chest and died.

His servant also thought Captain Morstan had (**7**) .... murdered and Major Sholto was (**8**) .... that the police might also think he was the murderer. He (**9**) .... the body and the treasure.

He asked his sons to (**10**) .... Captain Morstan's daughter half of the treasure after he died.

He wanted to tell them where the treasure was but, just at
(11) .... moment, he saw a face at the window and
(12) .... heart stopped beating.

3 Characters

Look at these sentences with the words from the text. Who says them?

1　'These two gentlemen are my friends.'　　　　................................

2　'I can tell you everything and I can also give　................................
　　you justice.'

3　'I have been a greedy man. At least half　　　................................
　　of the treasure belongs to her.'

4　'For many years he had a weak heart.'　　　　................................

5　'... all we found was a single footprint.'　　　................................

6　'That's why I moved out of Pondicherry Lodge.'　................................

Now match the sentences below to the sentences from the text in question 3.

A　☐　He had told Miss Morstan that her father was dead.

B　☐　He admitted that he had not treated Captain Morstan's
　　　　daughter well.

C　☐　He said he would tell them how Captain Morstan died.

D　☐　They had seen a face at the window and their father's heart
　　　　stopped beating.

E　☐　The man asked Miss Morstan to identify herself.

F　☐　He told them his brother did not want to give Miss Morstan her
　　　　share of the treasure.

4 What do you think?

Thaddeus Sholto appears to be an honest man, who wants to do the right thing and give Miss Morstan half of the treasure. Do you think he's genuine or could there be another reason for his actions?

5 Strange symbols

Major Sholto received a letter from India. The last part is written with some strange symbols.

Look at the symbols that are repeated most often (some letters are given to you as clues below). Can you guess what the other letters are? Rewrite the final part of the letter.

For the attention of Major Sholto.

You thought you were clever but you cannot hide. We know where you are. One of the four has escaped and will come and find you and take back what is ours.

⋂e   ⋂⇉ll   ⇶⃪⃪⃫e   s↵re   ⊢h⃪⇥   j↵s⇥⇶⃫e   ⇉s   ⃫o⃫e.

⋂e   ⋂⇉ll   f⇉⃫d   o↵⃕   ⇥⃕eas↵re   ⃪n⃫   yo↵   ⋂⇉ll   see

⋂G⃪⇥   G⃪↔⃪e⃫s   ⇥o   ⇥Gose   ⋂Go   do   no⇥   ⃕es↵e⃗⇥

o↵r   ⃪g⃕ee⃪⃗e⃫⇥.

⋂e   ⋂⇉ll   G⃪ve   our   ⃕eve⃫ge   an⃫   yo↵⃕   so⃫s   ⋂⇉ll

⃫eve⃕   be   ⃕⇉⇶⇉G.

Clues:

a = ⃪   d = ⃫   h = G   i = ⇉   m = ⃪   r = ⃕   t = ⇥   w = ⋂

Other symbols:

⃫ = ...   ⃪ = ...   ⃫ = ...   ↔ = ...   ↵ = ...

T: GRADE 7

6 Speaking: town and village life

1   What are the advantages of living in a big city like London? What are the disadvantages?

2   Do you think it's possible to have the same life in a city as in a village?

Before you read

1 Vocabulary

Read these descriptions and match them to the people.

A heiress   **B** housekeeper   **C** boxer   **D** cab driver

1 ☐ he/she takes people where they want to go
2 ☐ a servant who looks after a house
3 ☐ a man who fights as a sport
4 ☐ a woman who receives money after someone dies

2 Characters

Answer these questions about the people and what they do.

1 What is another word for cab driver? What sort of 'cab' did he drive in the story?
2 What jobs does a housekeeper do?
3 Who do you think is/was the boxer in the next part of the story?
4 Who is the heiress, do you think?

3 Listening

Listen to the first part of Chapter Four. Complete the text with the missing words.

The cab was (**1**) .... for us. On the (**2**) .... to Norwood, Thaddeus told us how Bartholomew had found out where the treasure was. He had (**3**) .... out the area of the house and realised that there was a (**4**) .... at the top of the house. He made a (**5**) .... in the ceiling which led to this space, and there was the treasure (**6**) .... He lowered it down (**7**) .... the hole into the room below.

'He thinks that the (**8**) .... are worth about half a (**9**) .... pounds,' said Thaddeus. We looked at each other. This (**10**) .... that Miss Morstan was rich. I am ashamed to say that I did not feel so (**11**) .... A poor doctor marrying an (**12**) .... was definitely out of the question.

CHAPTER **FOUR**

Murder at Pondicherry House

The cab was waiting for us. On the journey to Norwood, Thaddeus told us how Bartholomew had found out where the treasure was. He had worked out [1] the area of the house and realised that there was a space at the top of the house. He made a hole in the ceiling which led to this space, and there was the treasure chest. He lowered it down through the hole into the room below.

'He thinks that the jewels are worth about half a million pounds,' said Thaddeus.

We looked at each other. This meant that Miss Morstan was rich. I am ashamed to say that I did not feel so glad. A poor doctor marrying an heiress [2] was definitely out of the question.

It was nearly eleven o'clock when the cab stopped and we got out. 'This is Pondicherry House, Miss Morstan,' said Thaddeus.

---

1. **worked out** : calculated, found the solution to a problem.
2. **heiress** : name given to a female heir.

The house had a lot of land around it, which was all surrounded by a high stone wall. We waited at the gate.

'Who's there?' asked a voice from inside.

'McMurdo, it's me, Thaddeus. Let us in.'

The gate opened. McMurdo looked strong.

'Who are these people?' he asked. 'I can't let them in, sir, I don't know them.'

Sherlock Holmes stepped forward. 'I think you do, McMurdo. Do you remember that amateur boxer who fought with you a few years back?'

'Not Mr Sherlock Holmes!' cried McMurdo. 'Of course I remember you! Well, come on in. Sorry, Mr Thaddeus, but I had my orders.'

We followed Thaddeus up the path to the house.

'There's no light in Bartholomew's room,' said Thaddeus. 'How strange. He knows we're coming.'

'There's a light in that window there,' said Holmes, pointing.

'That's where Mrs Bernstone, the housekeeper, is,' said Thaddeus. 'I'll go in and speak to her. Wait here a moment.'

We saw the door open, and heard Mrs Bernstone crying.

'Oh, Mr Thaddeus, I'm so glad you're here!'

We waited outside. Miss Morstan and I stood together. She put her hand in mine. What a wonderful thing love is! We had met only that day, but it seemed so natural to be standing there with her, hand in hand.

Suddenly, the door opened and Thaddeus came running out.

'There's something wrong with Bartholomew!' he cried. 'I'm so scared!'

'Come into the house,' said Holmes, taking control of the situation.

We followed him in.

'Mr Bartholomew has locked himself in his room and won't answer me,' the housekeeper explained. 'I went up and looked through the keyhole — you must look for yourselves. I've never seen him look like that before.'

Holmes went upstairs. I followed, but Miss Morstan stayed with the frightened housekeeper.

We arrived at the door to Bartholomew's room. Holmes knocked: there was no reply. Then he tried to open it, but it was locked from the inside. He bent down to look through the keyhole.

He stood up again instantly, looking shocked.

'Have a look, Watson,' he said. 'What do you think?'

I looked through, then stepped back in horror. In the moonlight I saw a face, the very same face as Thaddeus with the same bald head. But there was a horrible smile on his face. I turned to make sure Thaddeus was still with us. Then I remembered that he and his brother were twins.

'This is terrible!' I said to Holmes. 'What do we do?'

'We must break down the door,' he replied.

We broke down the door and went into the room. It looked like a laboratory. There were some large containers. One of them was on its side and a small stream of dark liquid came from it. It smelt very strong, like tar.[1] In the middle of the room were some steps. Above them was a hole in the ceiling big enough for a man to get through. At the bottom of the steps was a rope.

Bartholomew Sholto was in the chair. He was stiff[2] and cold

1. **tar** : a dark sticky strong smelling liquid which comes from coal and wood.
2. **stiff** : hard, rigid.

44

and had obviously been dead for many hours. On the table was a note. Holmes picked it up.

'You see?' he said, giving it to me.

It read, 'The sign of the four.'

'What does it mean?' I asked him.

'It means murder,' he said. 'Look here.'

He pointed to a long thin dart [1] stuck in the skin of the dead man, just above his ear.

'Take it out,' he said to me, 'but be careful. It's poisoned.'

I took it out carefully. It was long, sharp and black. It looked like a thorn [2] but not from any tree in England.

'I don't understand. It becomes more complicated at every step.'

Holmes disagreed. 'It becomes clearer every minute. I just need a few missing clues,' he said. We had almost forgotten about Thaddeus since we entered the room. Suddenly he spoke.

'The treasure has gone!' he cried. 'They've taken the treasure! I helped him to bring it down through that hole last night. I was the last person to see him. I heard him lock the door behind me.'

'What time was that?' asked Holmes.

'About ten o'clock. And now he's dead and the police will think I killed him! It wasn't me! I didn't do it! You do believe me, don't you? Oh, I think I'm going mad!'

Holmes put his hand on his shoulder. 'Don't worry, Mr Sholto,' he said kindly. 'Go to the police station. Say you'll help them in any way you can. We'll wait here for you.'

---

1. **dart** : a long, thin object with a sharp point.
2. **thorn** : sharp point on some plants and trees.

The text and **beyond**

1 Summary

Make sentences about the events in Chapter Four by matching 1-8 with A-H. Write the second part below and put the completed sentences in the correct order to make a summary.

1 ☐ Holmes saw that Bartholomew

....

2 ☐ Thaddeus saw that

....

3 ☐ In the skin of the dead man there was

....

4 ☐ Bartholomew found out

....

5 ☐ Thaddeus went to

....

6 ☐ At first McMurdo did not want to let them in

....

7 ☐ On the table there was

....

8 ☐ Bartholomew had locked the door and so they

....

A had been dead for some hours.

B a note. It read the 'Sign of the Four'.

C where the treasure was.

D the police to tell them his story.

E but then he recognised Sherlock Holmes.

F the treasure had disappeared.

G looked in through the keyhole.

H a long thin poisoned dart.

2 What do you think?

Choose the answer closest to your opinion. Discuss your answer with another student, giving reasons for your opinion.

1   Why could Watson not marry Miss Morstan if she was rich?

A ☐ Rich women do not marry doctors.

B ☐ He was older than her. If she was rich she could choose any man she wanted.

C ☐ A woman married for wealth. If she was rich, she wouldn't need to marry.

2   How have times changed since late 18th-century Britain with regard to marriage?

A ☐ Today people are richer and so they have more choice and independence.

B ☐ A woman can look after herself and so she chooses a husband for love.

C ☐ Men and women marry the person they love. They never worry about money.

T: GRADE 7

3 Speaking: national customs

Describe the custom of marriage in your country. Answer the questions.

1   What is the minimum legal age to get married?

2   At what age do most people get married and for what reasons?

3   Do a woman's/man's parents ever arrange the marriage?

4   Do the woman's/man's family give the couple money for the wedding?

5   What do the couple — the bride and groom — usually wear?

6   Where do the couple usually go after the wedding ceremony?

4 Vocabulary

Read the descriptions of these words from Chapter Four and find them in the text.

1   a large garden outside a big house ....
2   a box for keeping clothes or other objects in ....
3   precious jewels or metal ....
4   to have no hair ....
5   the top part of a room ....
6   a small hole in the door to put a key in ....
7   a place for doing experiments ....
8   a black sticky liquid used on roads ....
9   used for tying things together ....
10 a sharp part of a plant ....
11 a small sharp object you throw ....

FCE 5 Hidden treasure and a mysterious map

You are going to read a famous legend about some hidden treasure. Four sentences have been removed. Choose the one that best fits each gap. Choose from the paragraphs A-E. There is one extra paragraph which you do not need to use. There is an example at the beginning (0).

Stories of hidden or missing treasure have fascinated readers for centuries.

0 ....D....

The Knights Templar were a group of monks and soldiers who fought in wars called 'the Crusades'. Their job was to protect people visiting the Holy Land — the area which is now Israel and Palestine — and to protect Christian sites. They also stole many precious objects from these sites.

1 ....

Some people believe that the secret of the treasure was also taken to America by the 'Founding Fathers' — the first Europeans to live there. They left a map of where to find the treasure on the back of an important document and left some clues on American bank notes.

2   ....

These theories, like many others, are probably untrue, but we love to hear about them anyway.

3   ....

Perhaps we will never know what these objects really are, or where they are hidden, but we can enjoy the idea that finding secret treasure could change the world.

A   Other people think that the treasure is hidden under a church in Scotland and there is a secret sign that indicates the place.

B   Many books have been written about the subject and there are several films. Some of the more recent ones include a film with Nicholas Cage, *National Treasure* (2004) and *The Da Vinci Code* (2006).

C   You can visit Rosslyn chapel, in Scotland, near Edinburgh, and see the beautiful work on the church, done by some men connected to the Knights Templar.

D   Perhaps one the world's most famous legends concerns some precious objects taken by a group of men called the Knights Templar from a temple in Jesusalem, including a cup known as 'The Holy Grail'.

E   The legend says that the Templars hid the 'treasure' for political reasons but they told their secret to certain people. It is a popular belief that a society of men called Freemasons now guard their secret.

T: GRADE 7

6 Speaking: early memories

Ask and answer these questions with another student.

1   When you were small, did you ever dream of finding treasure? How and where?

2   In what stories did you read about hidden treasure?

3   Did you ever join in a 'treasure hunt' (when someone hides objects and you look for them)?

CHAPTER FIVE

Holmes Gets to Work

N
ow, Watson,' said Holmes, 'we've got half an hour to find out what happened. So, how did these people come and go? The door hasn't been opened since last night. Let's look at the window. The window is locked on the inside. Let's open it. Nothing to climb up. The roof is too far away. But, a man did come in by the window last night. Here's a footprint. And here is a round muddy mark, and here, and here by the table. See Watson, it all becomes clear.'

I looked at the round marks. 'That's not a footprint,' I said.

'No, it's the mark made by a wooden leg,' he said.

'The wooden-legged man.'

'Exactly. But there has been someone else here. A very efficient partner. Look out of the window; is it possible to climb that wall, Watson?'

I looked out. 'Impossible,' I said. 'It's sixty feet [1] and there's nowhere to stand.'

---

1. **feet** : (here) a foot is a British unit of measurement equal to 30.48 centimetres. So, 60 feet = about 18 metres.

'Without help, it's impossible. But if there was someone in this room who drops a rope down from the window, like that rope over there, then I think even a wooden-legged man could climb up. Then he can leave the same way and the person in the room simply pulls the rope up, closes and locks the window. He gets out the same way he came in. Look at the end of the rope. There are marks of blood on it where the wooden-legged man took the skin from his hands when he went down.'

'Yes, but what about this mysterious partner?' I asked. 'How did he get into the room? The door is locked and you can't get to the window without help. Did he come down the chimney?'

'No,' said Holmes, 'it's too small. I'd already thought of that.'

'Well, how then?'

'Think, Watson! He didn't come through the door, the window or the chimney. There's nowhere for him to hide in the room. So what's left?'

'He came through the hole in the ceiling!' I cried.

'Of course he did,' said Holmes. 'There's no other way. Now, let's go up through the hole and have a look in the room where the treasure was hidden.'

The room was very small. There was no furniture but a lot of dust. Holmes found a trap door [1] that opened on to the roof of the house.

'This is how the partner, let's call him Number One, entered. Let's see if he has left any more clues.'

Holmes examined the floor. I saw a look of surprise on his face. I looked down. The floor was covered in footprints of a

---

1. **trap door** : a small door, usually in a ceiling or floor.

naked foot. They were very clear, but they were half the size of an ordinary footprint.

'Holmes,' I whispered, 'has a child done this terrible thing?'

'I was confused for a minute, but it can be explained. There's nothing more to be learned here. Let's go down again.'

I asked him what he thought about the small footprints.

'Watson, try to think of an answer for yourself. You know how I work. Try it yourself and we can compare results,' he said impatiently.

'I can't think of anything,' I answered.

'It'll become clear soon,' he said. 'I want to have a last look at this room now.'

He got out his magnifying glass and went carefully around the room, talking to himself. Finally, he stopped.

'We won't have any trouble now,' he said. 'Number One has stepped in the tar. You can see his small footprint here. This container was knocked over and the tar has leaked out.'

'And so?' I asked, still confused.

'We can find him,' said Holmes. 'I know a dog that can follow a smell anywhere, especially one as strong as tar.'

We heard some noise. The police had arrived.

'Before they get up here,' said Holmes, 'just feel the arm of the dead man. What do you think?'

I touched the arm of the dead man. The muscles were extremely hard.

'This is more than the usual rigor mortis. [1] It's from the poison. That's why his face has that strange smile on it.'

---

1. **rigor mortis** : the stiffness that occurs in a dead body.

'Exactly,' said Holmes. 'The poison from the dart. Now with all this information, you can begin to understand,' he said.

As he was speaking the police came into the room. One of them was a very fat, red faced man.

'Well, well,' he said, looking at the body. 'But who are you?'

'You must remember me, Mr Athelney Jones,' said Holmes quietly.

'Of course I do! It's Sherlock Holmes,' he said. 'You helped in that case at Bishopsgate; but you must admit it was more luck than your skill.'

'It was just some very simple reasoning,' said Holmes.

'Oh, don't be embarrassed to admit it! How lucky that I was out at Norwood investigating another case! I was at the station when the message arrived. What do you think the man died of?'

'Oh, this is hardly a case for me to investigate,' replied Holmes dryly.

'No, but I can't deny that you sometimes do get it right. So, what do you think has happened here, Holmes?' said Mr Jones. 'Door locked, jewels gone. Hmm. Ha! I've got it! The brother died in a fit[1] and Thaddeus Sholto walked off with the treasure. How about that?'

'And the dead man got up and locked the door from the inside?' said Holmes.

'Hmm! No, that can't be right.' Mr Athelney Jones continued talking to himself, looking around the room. He even went up into the room above, which was not easy for a man his size.

---

1. **fit** : sudden attack.

Eventually, he called to the policeman outside the room.

'Ask Mr Sholto to come in,' he said. 'Mr Sholto. I must tell you that anything you say will be used against you. I am arresting you for being involved in the death of your brother.'

'I knew it!' said poor Mr Sholto.

'Don't worry, Mr Sholto,' said Holmes. 'I promise you I can prove who really killed your brother.'

'Don't promise too much, Mr Holmes,' said Athelney Jones. 'It might be harder than you think.'

'Well, Mr Jones, I'll tell you the name and description of one of the two people who were in this room last night. His name is Jonathan Small. He has a wooden leg. He is middle aged, sunburnt and has been in prison. The other man is a rather unusual person. I hope that I will be able to bring them both to justice soon. Let's go, Watson.' Athelney Jones looked shocked.

On the stairs I told Holmes that it was time to take Miss Morstan home. He agreed.

'When you have taken Miss Morstan home, I want you to go to Pinchin Lane,' he said. 'The third house on the right belongs to Mr Sherman. Tell him that I need to borrow Toby. Bring Toby back here in the cab with you.'

'Toby is a dog?' I asked.

'Yes. He has the most powerful nose in London,' said Holmes. 'While you are away, I'll see what Mrs Bernstone can tell me.'

The text and **beyond**

1 Comprehension check

Decide if these sentences about Chapter Five are true (T) or false (F).
Correct the false ones.

		T	F
1	The victim left a footprint and the mark of a wooden leg.	☐	☐
2	The men used the rope to kill Bartholomew Sholto.	☐	☐
3	The 'partner' climbed into the room from the roof.	☐	☐
4	'Number One' stepped in the tar.	☐	☐
5	Holmes said the footprints were made by a child.	☐	☐
6	The dead man was smiling because he kept the secret of the treasure.	☐	☐
7	Athelney Jones's theory is not possible.	☐	☐
8	Athelney Jones arrested Thaddeus Sholto.	☐	☐

2 Deductions

Tick (✓) the conclusions. Some of them are wrong. Discuss in class.

A ☐ The man with the wooden leg shot Mr Sholto.
B ☐ Mr Sholto died from the poison in the dart.
C ☐ Both suspects came through a trapdoor.
D ☐ One man climbed a rope into the room.
E ☐ Jonathan Small was there because he left the mark of a wooden leg.
F ☐ The men killed Mr Sholto so they could steal the treasure.
G ☐ Number One climbed into the room from the roof.
H ☐ One of the men had very big footprints.

3 Characters

Why do you think Conan Doyle chose Watson as the narrator? Look at the following answers and put them in order from 1 (closest to your opinion) to 4 (furthest from your opinion).

A ☐ We are more likely to believe what Watson tells us than Holmes.

B ☐ Holmes knows everything. If Holmes told the story it would be very short and the author couldn't write a book about it.

C ☐ Holmes is arrogant and he would only write about himself, not other people.

D ☐ This way the author can hide some of the facts from us because Dr Watson doesn't know everything, just like us.

FCE ④ **Did Sherlock Holmes really exist?**

For questions 1-12, read the text below. Use the word in capitals at the end of each line to form a word that fits the space in the same line. There is an example (0) at the beginning.

Many people would like to know if Sherlock Holmes was part of Conan Doyle's (**0**) ...imagination..., or if he really (**1**)	**IMAGINE** **EXIST**
The answer to the second part of this question is 'yes'. He was Conan Doyle's professor.	
Joseph Bell was a professor of medicine at Edinburgh University. One day he (**2**) .... his class how it was possible to give a good (**3**) .... of a person and their past by simple (**4**)	**SHOW** **DESCRIBE** **OBSERVE**
A patient came into their class and he asked the man some questions. The man answered 'yes' to all of them and went away in (**5**)	**AMAZE**
Why? Because their professor had (**6**) .... guessed the man's job, his regiment, where he had been in the army, and that he had only just arrived in England. He then (**7**) .... how he had come to his (**8**)	**CORRECT** **EXPLAIN** **CONCLUDE**
'The man had good manners, but he did not take off his hat. A man does not (**9**) .... do this in the army, so he had not been out of the army long enough to remember to take it off. He was still (**10**) .... and his (**11**) .... is (**12**) .... found among soldiers in the West Indies. The Scottish soldiers there are in the Highlander Regiment, based in Barbados.'	**USUAL** **SUNTAN** **ILL / COMMON**
Elementary, my dear students!	

60

5 Speaking

Do you know any other famous detectives? Which detective books have you read in your own language? Describe them.

Use the table to make a list of the characteristics of the detectives and the books to help you.

Time book is set (e.g. 18th century)	The book is set in the
Author	
Some titles you know/have read	
Description of detective (clothes, habits etc.)	His/her name is... He/She wears a...
Methods of detection	(e.g. he guesses the criminal's next move by...)
Description of one of the criminals	In (title) there is a criminal called...

FCE ## 6 Report

You have been asked to write a report for a school newspaper on crime stories. Suggest which books are best (including the names of the detectives in them) and why you think people should read them. Write your report (120-180 words).

7 Crime quiz

Test your knowledge of crime and criminals with this quiz! You can check your answers on page 127.

1   When did the first policemen appear on the streets in England?

A ☐ 1829
B ☐ 1843
C ☐ 1861

2   In 1963, one of the biggest robberies ever took place in England. What was it called?

A ☐ The Great Train Robbery
B ☐ The Royal Mail Robbery
C ☐ The Bank of England Robbery

3 Which of these detectives can you read about in Agatha Christie's crime stories?

A ☐ Inspector Gadget.

B ☐ Inspector Clouseau.

C ☐ Inspector Poirot.

4 Which of these is the title of a famous book by a Russian author?

A ☐ *War and Crime.*

B ☐ *Crime and Punishment.*

C ☐ *Punishment and Criminals.*

5 Which of these is a famous criminal couple?

A ☐ Torville and Dean.

B ☐ Bonnie and Clyde.

C ☐ Fred and Ginger.

6 Which criminal was in the 2001 film *From Hell* with Johnny Depp in it?

A ☐ the Mafia boss Don Corleone

B ☐ a cannibal called Hannibal Lector

C ☐ the murderer Jack the Ripper

Before you read

1 Reading pictures

Look at the picture on pages 68-69 and answer the questions.

1 Where are Watson and Holmes?

2 What do you think they are doing?

3 What do you think they will find?

CHAPTER **SIX**

Following the Trail ¹

I took Miss Morstan home in the cab. The adventures of this strange night had become too much for her and she began to cry. She has told me since that she thought I was cold and distant on this night. But I did not want to take advantage of her. She was tired and weak and she was also rich; how could I tell her I loved her at such a time? It did not seem fair, although it was very difficult not to comfort her as I wanted to.

I left her with Mrs Forrester and continued on my journey.

The cab arrived at Pinchin Lane. I knocked at the door. A voice shouted from a window above.

'Go away or I'll let out the dogs.'

'It's a dog that I want,' I began, but I was interrupted again.

'Go on, if you don't go away, I'll —'

---

1. **trail** : a series of marks left by someone or something.

'Mr Sherlock Holmes —' I interrupted, and the words had their usual magical effect.

In a minute, the door opened, and Mr Sherman invited me in.

'Now, what was it that Mr Sherlock Holmes wanted, sir?'

'He wants a dog of yours — Toby,' I replied.

Toby appeared. He was an ugly dog, brown and white with long hair. He followed me into the cab and we left. We arrived back at Pondicherry House at about three in the morning.

'Ah, there's Toby! Good dog,' said Holmes. 'Athelney Jones has arrested Thaddeus, the servant and the housekeeper! So we have the house to ourselves at the moment. Leave Toby there for a minute. I'm going to climb out of that trap door and go onto the roof. You go outside and look out for me.'

By the time I got out into the area around the house, Holmes was out on the roof.

'Is that you, Watson?' he shouted.

'Yes.'

'This is the place where he got down. Is there a ladder?'

'No.'

'Oh well, I must be able to climb down this water pipe. Here I come.'

He landed on the ground. 'There,' he said. 'It was easy to see where Number One had been. There were loose parts on the roof where he walked, and he dropped this.'

He held out a small purse; inside were another six or seven of the poisoned darts.

'So, are you ready for a long walk, Watson?'

'Oh, yes,' I replied.

'Here you are, doggy! Good boy, Toby! Smell it, Toby, smell it!' Holmes held out a cloth that he had put in the tar and let Toby

sniff it. Holmes then threw the cloth away and led Toby to the water barrel. Toby immediately became very excited and rushed off with his nose to the ground and his tail in the air. It was difficult to keep up with him. [1]

It was beginning to get light. Toby led us across the grounds to a place in the wall. It was easy to climb. Holmes went first and then I passed Toby to him and he dropped the dog over the other side.

'It's lucky for us that it hasn't rained. Toby will be able to follow the tar smell easily,' said Holmes.

It seemed to be true. Toby did not hesitate, he just kept his nose to the ground. As we followed him, I asked Holmes how he was so sure about the wooden-legged man.

'My dear Watson! It's so simple. Two soldiers are in charge of a prison. They find out about some secret treasure. An Englishman named Jonathan Small draws a map for them. You remember that name was on Captain Morstan's map. Jonathan Small signed it for himself and his friends — the sign of the four. With the help of this map, the two officers — or one of them, Major Sholto — gets the treasure and brings it to England. He didn't do what he was supposed to do for the group of four. Now, why didn't Jonathan Small and his friends get the treasure themselves? Because they were in prison: they couldn't get to the treasure.

'So, Major Sholto is quite happy with his treasure for some years in England. Then he receives a letter from India which frightens him. It says that the men of the sign of the four have been set free or that they have escaped. So now Major Sholto looks out for a wooden-legged man — a white man because he

---

1. **keep up with him** : go as fast as him.

mistakes a salesman for him and even fires his gun at him. Now only one white man's name is on the map. The other names are Hindu or Muslim. There is no other white man. So that means that the wooden-legged man is Jonathan Small. Does that make sense?'

I agreed that it did.

'So, let's pretend we are Jonathan Small. He comes to England with two things on his mind. One, to get his treasure and two, having his revenge on [1] Major Sholto. He finds out where Sholto lives. But he doesn't know where the treasure is hidden. Only the major knows. Small hears that the major is very ill. He must find out where the treasure is before he dies, so he goes to the window of Major Sholto's room. But he doesn't go in because the two sons are there. He comes back later and searches the room, hoping to find something which will tell him where the treasure is. He finds nothing but decides to leave the note with 'The sign of the four' on it. To him, it's like an act of justice for him and his friends.

'Now what did Jonathan Small do? He waited until the treasure was discovered; but he needs help because he can't get to the room with his wooden leg.'

'Number One,' I said. 'He murdered Bartholomew Sholto.'

'Yes, and I don't think Jonathan Small was pleased about that. He just wanted to frighten him. There was no need to kill him. But his friend's savage instincts led him to kill Bartholomew Sholto. So Jonathan Small takes the treasure and leaves.'

I understood so far. 'And Number One?'

'Well, that will become clear soon,' said Holmes. 'Now, where are we?'

---

1. **having his revenge on** : punishing.

We had followed Toby to Knight's Place. Here, Toby stopped and began running backwards and forwards, and around in circles. He looked up at us continuously .

'What's the matter with this dog?' asked Holmes.

Suddenly, Toby seemed to find the scent again and we

followed him down another small street. Toby ran down it, between two piles of wood, and stopped by a big container which stood on a cart. The cart was covered in a dark liquid and the air was full of the smell of tar.

Holmes and I looked at each other. Then we both started to laugh.

The text and **beyond**

FCE **1   Comprehension check**

For questions 1-8 choose the answer — A, B, C or D — which you think fits best according to the text.

1 How did Miss Morstan feel about Dr Watson's behaviour?

A ☐ That he was weak.

B ☐ That he was cold and distant.

C ☐ That she did not feel comfortable near him.

D ☐ That he did not love her as she wanted him to.

2 When did Watson arrive at Pondicherry House with Toby?

A ☐ just after he left Miss Morstan

B ☐ three hours after he left Pinchin Lane

C ☐ in the middle of the day

D ☐ in the early hours of the morning

3 Why did Holmes and Watson have the house to themselves?

A ☐ The housekeeper was not there.

B ☐ Bartholomew Sholto was dead.

C ☐ Athelney Jones had arrested everyone who lived in the house.

D ☐ No one wanted to go in the house after what had happened.

4 Why did Jonathan Small not get the treasure according to Holmes?

A ☐ Major Sholto hid it in England.

B ☐ Its location was a secret.

C ☐ He and his friends were in prison.

D ☐ His friends took the treasure for themselves.

5 How did Holmes know that one of the two suspects was Jonathan Small?

A ☐ All the other names were Hindu or Muslim.

B ☐ He was the only white man with a wooden leg.

C ☐ He was the salesman that Major Sholto shot at.

D ☐ He was the only white man to escape.

6 What did Jonathan Small hope to find in Major Sholto's house?
   A ☐ That the Major was dead.
   B ☐ Something to tell him where the treasure was.
   C ☐ A note from his friend with the Sign of Four.
   D ☐ Justice.

7 Who murdered Bartholomew Sholto?
   A ☐ Jonathan Small.
   B ☐ Jonathan Small's friend.
   C ☐ Thaddeus Sholto.
   D ☐ Mr Sherman.

8 What did Toby find?
   A ☐ The two men hiding in a container.
   B ☐ Number One behind two piles of wood.
   C ☐ A cart full of tar.
   D ☐ Another dog in a street.

2 Vocabulary

Miss Morstan thought Watson was 'cold and distant', when he wanted to be warm and caring and close to her. Match these adjectives to their opposites.

1 ☐ patient   A arrogant
2 ☐ honest   B weak
3 ☐ greedy   C generous
4 ☐ humble   D impatient
5 ☐ nervous   E naive
6 ☐ interesting   F dull
7 ☐ strong   G calm
8 ☐ wise   H dishonest

3 Characters

Choose five adjectives to describe at least three different people in this story.

9 **4** **Listening**

FCE

You will hear Mr Sherman talking to Watson. Complete the sentences.

1 He thought Watson was ....

2 The man once saw Holmes when ....

3 Sometimes people complain ....

4 Holmes can have ....

5 Toby can smell .... for miles.

6 The dog never ....

7 He's .... sniffer dog this side of ....

Before you read

1 **Vocabulary**

Match the words to their definitions. Then write the words in the puzzle to find out where Toby takes them.

A steam   **B** hire   **C** trail   **D** lovely   **E** sign

1 ☐ a path taking you to a place

2 ☐ a piece of wood with an advert or information

3 ☐ very nice in a sweet or pretty way

4 ☐ vapour from hot water

5 ☐ to rent something for a period of time

1 ☐☐☐☐☐
2 ☐☐☐☐
3 ☐☐☐☐☐☐
4 ☐☐☐☐
5 ☐☐☐☐

Answer: ☐☐☐☐☐

2 Reading pictures

Look at the picture on page 75 and answer the questions.

1 Who is Holmes talking to?

2 Who do you think she is?

3 What is the little boy doing?

4 What question do you think Holmes asks the woman?

3 Listening

Listen to the first part of Chapter Seven. Choose the best answer – A, B or C.

1 Who did Holmes and Watson see?
   A ☐ a woman advertising boat hire
   B ☐ a woman and a child near the boat house
   C ☐ a man called Mordecai Smith

2 Who had the woman's husband gone away with?
   A ☐ their little boy
   B ☐ a man called Jack
   C ☐ a wooden-legged man

3 What colour was the boat?
   A ☐ black with two red stripes
   B ☐ black and green
   C ☐ green and yellow

4 What do Holmes and Watson do next?
   A ☐ They ask the boy to take them across the river.
   B ☐ They hire a small boat.
   C ☐ They return to Baker Street in a cab.

5 Who does Holmes say can help them?
   A ☐ the woman's husband
   B ☐ the post office
   C ☐ the 'street boys'

73

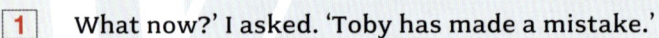

CHAPTER **SEVEN**

The Baker Street Boys

1 **What now?'** I asked. 'Toby has made a mistake.'

'There's a lot of tar used in London these days,' said Holmes. 'It's not surprising that he got confused. We'll take him back to the place where he followed the wrong trail.'

We walked back to Knight's Place. Toby then took us down a street which brought us to the edge of the river.

'Well, that's it,' said Holmes, 'they've taken a boat from here.'

Nearby was a small house with a sign. It said: 'Mordecai Smith, boats to hire by the hour or day.'

2 Sherlock Holmes walked towards the house. A small boy came running out. He was followed by a large red-faced woman.

'Come back here, Jack!' she shouted. Jack took no notice.

'What a lovely little boy,' said Sherlock Holmes. 'A fine child, Mrs Smith!'

'He is, sir, but he's difficult to manage, especially when my husband is away,' she said.

'Oh, is he away?' asked Holmes, 'I wanted to speak to him.'

'He's been away since yesterday morning, sir; I'm starting to

worry about him. He went away with that wooden-legged man. I don't like him.'

3   'A wooden-legged man?' said Holmes, pretending to be surprised.

'Yes, he came late last night and woke my husband up. I heard his wooden leg clicking on the road. They left in the steamboat.'

'I'm sorry to hear that, Mrs Smith, because I wanted to hire a steamboat. Is it that old green and yellow boat I've seen here? Let me think, what was it called?'

'Oh, no, sir, the *Aurora* has just been painted: it's black with two red stripes now.'

'Thanks. Well, I hope you hear from your husband, Mrs Smith. I'm going down the river. If I see him, I'll tell him you're worried about him. Ah, look, here's a small boat for hire. Let's go across to the other side of the river, Watson. Goodbye, Mrs Smith.'

4   On our way across the river, we decided what to do next.

'So are we going to search for the *Aurora*?' I asked.

'No, no,' said Holmes. 'That will take far too long.'

'Well, what do we do then?' I asked.

'We'll go home, have some breakfast and get some rest. We'll stop at the post office. I want to send a telegram to Wiggins. Do you remember how the street boys [1] helped in the Jefferson Hope case?'

5   We returned to Baker Street. I felt much better after a bath and some breakfast. We were reading the report of the case in the newspaper when the street boys arrived.

'Got your message, sir,' said Wiggins.

'Right, Wiggins. Here's a coin for each of you. I want you to find a steamboat called the *Aurora*, owned by a Mordecai Smith,

1. **street boys** : homeless children who survive by asking people for money.

black with two red stripes. It's on the river somewhere. Let me know as soon as you have any news. Is that clear?'

'Yes, sir,' said Wiggins.

'Very well. You can go now,' he said.

The boys left.

6 'Are you going to sleep, Holmes?' I asked him.

'No, no,' he replied. 'I want to think over this curious case. Wooden-legged men are not common, and the other man must be unique.'

'Yes, what about this other man, Number One?'

'You must have your own thoughts, Watson. Small footprints, naked feet, poison darts: what do you think?'

'An Indian!' I exclaimed. 'One of the Indians who were the friends of Jonathan Small?'

'I did consider that,' said Holmes, 'but no. Look at this.'

He turned the pages of a book.

'Here we are. 'The Andaman Islands. 340 miles to the north of Sumatra, in the Bay of Bengal. The aborigines of the Andaman Islands are perhaps the smallest people on earth. The average height is below four feet. Their feet and hands are very small. They are a very fierce group of people and fight using poisoned darts. They often eat their victims. What nice, friendly people, Watson!'

'But how did Jonathan Small and this aborigine become friends?' I asked.

'I don't know, Watson. Jonathan Small was on the Andaman Islands so he probably made friends with an islander. Anyway, Watson, you look tired. Why don't you go to sleep?'

I did as he suggested. Soon, I was dreaming about the sweet face of Miss Mary Morstan.

7   I woke up late in the afternoon feeling much better. Sherlock Holmes was reading a book.

'Have you heard anything?' I asked.

'No,' he answered. He sounded disappointed. 'I expected to know something by now. Wiggins was here while you were asleep. He says they can't find the boat.'

'Is there anything I can do?' I asked.

'No,' he replied, 'we just have to wait. You do what you want. I'll wait here.'

'Then I'll go over and see Mrs Cecil Forrester.'

'Mrs Cecil Forrester?' said Holmes, smiling.

'Well, of course, to see Miss Morstan as well. They were anxious to hear what happened. I'll be back in an hour or two.'

'Well, if you're going across the river you can take Toby back. I don't think we'll need him again.'

8   I took Toby back to Pinchin Lane and went to see Miss Morstan. The two women were very interested to hear what had happened.

'Just think, Mary,' said Mrs Forrester, 'if the search is successful, you'll be a rich woman!'

The text and **beyond**

1 Summary

Chapter Seven has been divided into eight parts. Choose from the list
(A-I) the sentence which best summarises each part. There is one
extra sentence which you do not need to use.

A ☐ Holmes and Watson discuss their next move.

B ☐ It is better to have friends than enemies.

C ☐ Watson brings Miss Morstan some interesting news.

D ☐ Watson learns more about the 'little friend'.

E ☐ A missing husband and a worried wife.

F ☐ There is nothing Holmes can do except wait.

G ☐ After a bad start, Toby gets it right.

H ☐ Holmes has a job for the street boys.

I ☐ A step closer to finding the wooden-legged man.

2 Comprehension check

Read these sentences. Which ones can you answer from what you
know from the story so far? Put a tick (✓). Which ones remain a
mystery? Put a cross (✗). Answer all the questions which have a tick
(✓).

1 ☐ How did Captain Morstan die?

2 ☐ Why does Jonathan Small have a wooden leg?

3 ☐ Who is Number One?

4 ☐ Who are the members of the 'Sign of the Four'?

5 ☐ Why does the treasure belong to the 'Sign of the Four'?

6 ☐ Who did it belong to originally?

7 ☐ How did Holmes find the two men?

8 ☐ Where is the treasure now?

3 What do you think?

Using the information you have, try and guess the answers to these questions.

1   Who killed Batholomew Sholto? How?

2   How did Jonathan Small meet the native from the Andaman Islands?

3   Why did they want Mordecai Smith's boat?

FCE 4 What do you think?

For questions 1-12 below, read the summary of Chapter Seven and think of the word which best fits each space. Use only one word in each space. There is an example at the beginning (0).

Toby took Holmes and Watson down (0) ...to............... the edge of the river where they saw a small house (1) .... a sign. The sign said 'Mordecai Smith, boats to hire (2) .... the hour or day.'

A small boy and a woman came out (3) .... the house and when Holmes asked to be able to speak to (4) .... husband, she explained that he had gone away the (5) .... day with a wooden-legged man. She told them that he had gone away in the *Aurora* — a black steamboat (6) .... two red stripes.

They returned to Baker Street and after breakfast the Baker Street boys arrived. Holmes gave them (7) .... money and told them to look for the *Aurora* on the river. After they (8) .... gone Holmes explained to Watson that the small footprints they had seen at the scene of the crime had been (9) .... by a native of the Andaman Islands. These natives were very small and fought by (10) .... poisoned darts.

Watson slept in the afternoon and when he woke up he found Holmes reading a book and (11) .... waiting for news. Watson decided to go and see Miss Morstan and Mrs Forrester to inform them of what had happened (12) .... far.

The British in India

Some of the events towards the end of *The Sign of Four* take place in India, which was known as 'the jewel in the crown' of the British Empire. The British Empire is the name given to the lands which Britain ruled from the late 17th century to the mid-20th century. In the late 19th century, the Empire included India, Burma (modern Myanmar), Australia, New Zealand, Canada, many islands in the Caribbean, Nigeria and South Africa. Most of these countries became independent after the end of World War II, in the period from 1945 to 1964; they are now part of the Commonwealth of Nations, a group of nations that includes the UK and the former colonies of the Empire.

India's connection with Britain began on 31 December 1600, when Queen Elizabeth I of England gave permission for a new company to trade [1] with the 'East Indies'. At this time what the Europeans called the 'East Indies' included the whole of South East Asia to the east of and including India. This new company, called the English East India Company, wanted to establish a permanent base in India. At first, rulers in India did not give their permission, but by 1700 the Company had trading ports in the important cities of Madras, Calcutta and Bombay (modern Mumbai).

The Company soon wanted more than the right to trade in India; it wanted land. It had its own army, and its commander Robert Clive defeated the forces of its rival, [2] the French East India Company. Then, in 1757, Clive attacked and defeated the forces of the ruler of the rich north-eastern area of Bengal. From this time, the English

---

1. **trade** : buy and sell things.
2. **rival** : a person or organisation that tries to do the same things in the same area.

The Relief of Lucknow (1859) by Thomas Jones Barker.
The British in the city of Lucknow in northern India were under siege from about 8,000 mutineers from 30 May till 27 November 1857. The painting shows their rescue by a British army.

East India Company became the strongest European trading company in India, and later it became the instrument of British colonial rule in India.

Most Indians did not like being forced to have new laws and a new religion, Christianity: they had their own religions, such as Hinduism and Islam. A crisis came in 1857, when the Indian soldiers in the Company's army were given a new kind of cartridge; [1] these cartridges were covered with pig and cow fat to make it easy to put into their rifles. For different reasons, this was offensive to both Hindus and Muslims: in the Hindu religion the cow is sacred, while in the Muslim religion the pig is an unclean animal.

---

1. **cartridge** : bullet.

In the event known as the 'Indian Mutiny' [1] (1857-58), the Indian soldiers of the Company's army killed their British officers and took Delhi, then the most important city in India. After this the mutineers [2] took other cities in India and killed the British soldiers there. The events narrated in the last chapter of *The Sign of Four* take place in the context of the Indian Mutiny.

British forces recaptured Delhi in 1857, and in the next year the mutineers all over India were, with great violence, defeated. The British government took over the rule of India from the East India Company, and in 1858 the British Raj started in India. 'Raj' is a word from Hindi (the Indian language with most speakers) which means the control of a country by a king or queen. Queen Victoria of Britain was made 'Empress of India' in 1877.

But, despite the modernisations such as the railway and postal services, and the education system, most Indians wanted independence. In 1920 the great pacifist Mahatma Gandhi (1869-1948) started a campaign [3] for independence. Finally, in 1947, Britain created two independent states: Pakistan in the north, where most people were Muslim, and India, where most people were Hindu. In the first weeks of independence, however, over a million people were killed when Muslims and Hindus attacked each other.

But from these difficult beginnings, India has now become the world's largest democracy with a population of 1.1 billion. In modern India you can still see the effect of the British Raj in large public buildings, the education system and the wide use of English.

---

1. **Mutiny** : an event when people (usually soldiers or sailors) refuse to obey the person who has authority.
2. **mutineers** : people who take part in a mutiny.
3. **campaign** : a number of activities, over a period time, to try to get political changes.

***The Great India Peninsula Railway Terminus and
Administrative Office, Bombay*** (1878) by Axel Herman Haig.
The British called this city Bombay, but in 1995 its name was changed back to
Mumbai, the name it had before the British came.

1 **Comprehension check**

Answer the following questions.

1 The Commonwealth of Nations is sometimes called just 'the Commonwealth'. What is it?

2 What were the 'East Indies'?

3 What was the English East India Company?

4 What caused the Indian Mutiny?

5 What happened after the Indian Mutiny?

6 When and how did India become independent?

7 What can you see in modern India that shows it was once part of the British Empire?

INTERNET PROJECT

Connect to the Internet and go to www.blackcat-cideb.com or www.cideb.it. Insert the title or part of the title of the book into our search engine. Open the page for *The Sign of Four*. Click on the Internet project link.

The first painting shows British soldiers leaving London to fight in the Indian Mutiny and the second painting shows them when they return.

▶ Click on 'The Introduction' at the top of the page. Why was the Indian Mutiny 'shocking'?

▶ Click on 'The Characters' and follow the instructions. How many of the characters in the first painting are in the second painting? Who has changed most?

▶ Click on 'The Costume' and follow the instructions. What interests you most? Tell the class.

How are returning war veterans treated in modern art and in the media?

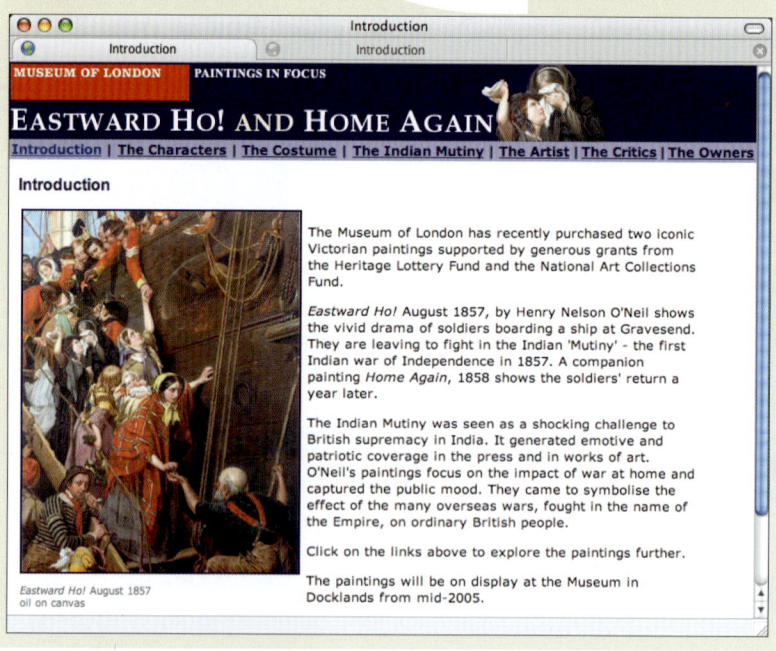

CHAPTER EIGHT

Chasing the Aurora

It was dark when I returned to Baker Street. Sherlock Holmes **11** had gone to his room. All night I heard him walking up and down.

The next morning at breakfast, he looked tired.

'I can't sleep,' he said. 'We are so close to solving this mystery but the boat can't be found.'

We heard nothing all that day either.

Early the next morning, I woke up and was surprised to see Sherlock Holmes standing by my bed. He was dressed as a sailor with a jacket and a red scarf around his neck.

'I'm going to the river, Watson. I've been thinking, and there's one thing left to try.'

'Can I come with you?' I asked.

'No,' he replied, 'I want you to stay here. Wiggins may come

with news. If any notes or telegrams arrive, then open them and do what you think is best.' He left.

It was a long day. No news came. I tried to read but could not concentrate. I wondered if for the first time Holmes had got it all wrong.

At about three o'clock, Athelney Jones came to the house. He had received a telegram from Holmes telling him to go to Baker Street.

We heard someone coming slowly up the stairs. An old man in sailor clothes came in. He had thick white eyebrows and a long grey beard.

'Can I help you?' I asked him.

'Is Mr Sherlock Holmes here?' he asked.

I told the old man that he was out.

'But you can give any messages to me,' I said.

'No, I have to tell Sherlock Holmes,' said the old man.

'Well, you must wait for him then. Is it about Mordecai Smith's boat?' I asked.

The old man said that it was and that he knew all about the treasure as well. He did not want to wait, but Mr Athelney Jones told him that he had to. The old man sat down and we continued with our conversation and our cigars.

After a few moments, we heard Sherlock Holmes' voice.

'Is there a cigar for me too?' he said.

We both jumped.

'Holmes!' I said. 'But where is the old man?'

'Here is the old man!' he said, holding out some white hair. 'I

thought my disguise was pretty good, but not that good,' he laughed. 'I have been working like this all day. How are you, Mr Jones?' he asked.

Athelney Jones shook his head.

'Not good. I had to release two of my suspects.'

'Don't worry,' said Holmes. 'If you do as I say, we'll have two more prisoners for you. You can take all the credit but you must do as I say.'

Athelney Jones agreed.

'I'll need a fast police boat to be at Westminster at seven o'clock, and two strong men,' said Holmes. 'When we catch the men, we'll get the treasure. I'm sure Watson here wants to take the box around to Miss Morstan. Half of it is hers after all. I want an unofficial interview with Jonathan Small. And you must stay for dinner, Mr Jones.'

Soon it was time to go. Holmes told me to take my pistol. We arrived at the river at Westminster and our boat was waiting for us. Holmes told the police to stop opposite Jacobson's Yard. ¹ On the way, he told me what had happened.

'Watson, I have been thinking. Jonathan Small and his friend from the Andaman Islands are very noticeable so they do everything by night. They pay Mordecai Smith well to keep the *Aurora* ready for them. Then they wait a night or two. Then when they think it's safe, they take the boat to Gravesend where they probably have tickets on a ship for America. That's what they're going to do tonight.'

---

1. **Yard** : (here) large open area where boats are made and repaired.

'But what about the *Aurora*?' I asked. 'Why hasn't it been found? It's not easy to hide a boat.'

'No,' agreed Holmes. 'That's why we're going to Jacobson's Yard. The men have taken the boat to a boat builder and told them to make a small repair. The boat is now hidden inside one of their buildings. I asked at several boat builders until I found the *Aurora* at Jacobson's. The man told me that there was nothing wrong with the boat. I was there when Mordecai Smith arrived. He was drunk. He told the man that he wanted the *Aurora* at eight o'clock tonight. So, I've left one of the street boys watching the boat. We'll wait out in the water on our police boat and I'll be surprised if we don't get the boat, the two men and the treasure this evening.'

It was dark when we arrived at the yard. We waited out in the water.

'There's the *Aurora*!' shouted Holmes suddenly. 'It's going very fast! Come on! Follow that boat!'

'I think they're going too fast!' said Athelney Jones. 'I don't think we can catch them!'

'We must catch them!' said Holmes. 'Come on!'

Slowly we came closer to the *Aurora*. We were getting closer and closer when a large boat pulling three smaller ones came between us and the *Aurora*. By the time we had gone around them, the *Aurora* was further ahead. But we continued as fast as we could. Athelney Jones put our search light on the *Aurora*. Now they knew we were following them.

Athelney Jones shouted at them to stop. The man in the back of the *Aurora* stood up and made an angry gesture in our

direction. He was a tall powerful man and I saw that he had a wooden leg. Next to him, a small man stood up, the smallest man I have ever seen. Holmes already had his gun out and I took out my pistol.

'If he raises his hand, fire,' said Holmes quietly.

Our boat was now next to theirs. We saw the tiny man take out a short round piece of wood and put it to his lips. Holmes and I fired together. The small man threw his hands up and fell into the river. The other man turned the *Aurora* suddenly, and went towards the bank. [1] It was a very muddy [2] area. The *Aurora* hit the bank and the wooden-legged man tried to climb onto the land. But his wooden leg immediately sank in the mud. He could not go forward or backward. He was stuck.

We pulled him out of the mud and onto our boat. Mordecai Smith also came on board our boat. On the *Aurora* there was a heavy iron chest; it was the treasure. We took it onto our boat and tied the *Aurora* behind us. We went slowly up the river again. We moved our lights over the river looking for the man from the Andaman Islands. But there was no sign of him.

'Look,' said Holmes. 'We were only just quick enough with our pistols.'

I looked. Behind us was a poisoned dart, stuck in the wood of our boat.

---

1. **bank** : (here) side of the river.
2. **muddy** : covered in mud; a mixture of earth and water.

The text and **beyond**

1 Comprehension check

For questions 1-6 choose the answer — A, B, C or D — which you think fits best according to the text.

1   Why was Holmes dressed as a sailor?

   A ☐ He wanted to go out and find the boat.

   B ☐ He wanted to look like the suspect.

   C ☐ He wanted to play a trick on Athelney Jones.

   D ☐ He didn't want Wiggins to know who he was.

2   Why was Athelney Jones at the house?

   A ☐ He had received a telegram about the men.

   B ☐ He had followed the street boys.

   C ☐ Wiggins had told him to come.

   D ☐ He had received a telegram from Holmes.

3   Why did the two men do everything at night?

   A ☐ It was easier to hide the treasure at night.

   B ☐ It would be too easy to recognise them during the day.

   C ☐ Mordecai Smith gave them the boat at night.

   D ☐ The boat was being repaired during the day.

4   Where did the two men probably want to escape to?

   A ☐ The Andaman Islands

   B ☐ Jacobson's Yard

   C ☐ America

   D ☐ Gravesend

5   Why did Holmes and Watson shoot at the small man?

   A ☐ He wanted to fire a dart at them.

   B ☐ He wanted to jump into the river.

   C ☐ He had a sharp piece of wood.

   D ☐ He ran for the shore.

6 What was on the boat?

A ☐ the missing treasure

B ☐ a box for Miss Morstan

C ☐ a dead man

D ☐ a bag of poisoned darts

FCE ❷ A letter

You receive this letter about a request you made to hire a boat on the Thames for a party with yourself and twelve friends. Read the letter, then using all the information in your notes, write a suitable reply in 120-180 words.

Dear Miss Jones

Thank you for your enquiry about hiring a Thames River boat.

The cost is £25 per person on the night cruise with buffet. Some drinks are included. The boat takes you and your party from the Embankment, near the Embankment underground station at 8.00 pm to Tower Bridge and returns at 11.30 pm.

To make a reservation, please send us a cheque for 10% of the total amount.   *send cheque*

We will also need some additional details from you.

Tell them!

• Please give us your full name and address.

• Please tell us how many people will be in your group.   *10*

• Would you like us to organise entertainment, e.g. a DJ, a comedian? (additional cost - price depends on the type of entertainment)   *DJ how much?*

• Does anyone in your party have special requests, e.g. vegetarian menu?

vegetarians

Regards

Brian O'Toole (Group Organiser)

3 Setting

Can you remember these places in the story? Name at least one thing that happened in each place and the reason for going there. There is an example at the beginning (0).

0 The Lyceum Theatre
Miss Morstan went with Holmes and Watson to meet the man who had sent her the letter. She wanted to meet the man to find out about her father.

1 The oriental looking house.

2 Pondicherry House.

3 Pinchin Lane.

4 The house by the river.

5 Mrs Cecil Forrester's house.

4 Vocabulary – means of transport

Look at these pictures and describe the means of transport.
Which verbs can you use with each method of transport? Use the verbs plus a preposition from the box.

> get + into/out of/on/off   travel + on (a)/in (a)/by

1 .... **2** .... **3** ....

4 .... **5** .... **6** ....

96

12

FCE

5 Listening

You will hear five people talking about transport. For each question, choose the opinion that each speaker expresses. Use the letters only once. There is one extra letter which you do not need to use.

Speaker

A   Travelling by camel is uncomfortable.   1 ☐

B   I don't like using public transport.   2 ☐

C   I use my car because if I didn't, I couldn't go anywhere.   3 ☐

D   I prefer trains to planes.   4 ☐

E   It's not comfortable, but it's quick.   5 ☐

F   I would like to live on a boat.

6 Speaking

Make a list of different methods of transport. Compare and discuss the methods on your list with another student; e.g. Which are quicker? Which are better for the environment? etc.

Before you read

13

1 Listening

Listen to the first part of Chapter Nine. Answer true (T) or false (F).

		T	F
1	Tonga was the name of the little man.	☐	☐
2	Jonathan Small murdered Bartholomew Sholto.	☐	☐
3	Mordecai Smith knew nothing of the murder.	☐	☐
4	The boat was going to take them to a place where they could escape.	☐	☐
5	The key to the treasure was in Baker Street.	☐	☐
6	They stopped at Mrs Cecil Forrester's house first.	☐	☐
7	Watson told the policeman about the poisoned dart.	☐	☐
8	The Agra treasure was in the iron box.	☐	☐

CHAPTER NINE

The Sign of the Four

Jonathan Small now sat in our boat with us.

'I'm sorry that it has come to this,' said Sherlock Holmes.

'So am I,' he said. 'I promise you I never hurt Mr Sholto. It was that little mad man Tonga who shot one of his darts into him.'

'Have a cigar,' said Holmes. 'You are going to come up to my rooms and tell me everything. I think I can help you; I think I can prove that the poison acts so quickly that Bartholomew Sholto was dead before you even entered the room.'

'He was, sir. I was ready to kill Tonga for what he did, but he ran off. This treasure has brought nothing but trouble to anyone who has ever owned it.'

Athelney Jones returned from questioning Mordecai Smith.

'He says he knew nothing about the Norwood murder,' he said.

Our prisoner agreed. 'No, we told him nothing, we just paid him a lot of money for the use of his boat. He was to get more money if we arrived at our ship at Gravesend. It was going to Brazil.'

The Sign of Four

'Doctor Watson, we'll take you to Vauxhall Bridge. You take the treasure back to Baker Street. Where is the key?' he asked Jonathan Small.

'At the bottom of the river,' he replied.

I landed in Vauxhall and took a cab. A policeman came with me. We stopped at Mrs Cecil Forrester's house first.

Miss Morstan was there alone. I went in with the box and put it on the table.

Miss Morstan looked at the iron box.

'Is that the treasure then?' she asked.

'Yes, this is the Agra treasure. Half of it is yours and half is Thaddeus Sholto's. You'll have a couple of hundred thousand each. Just think of that! You'll be one of the richest young ladies in England!'

'If I am, it is because of you,' she said simply.

'Not me; Sherlock Holmes,' I said.

'Tell me all about it, Doctor Watson,' she asked. She went white when I told her about the poisoned dart.

'It's all over. There is the treasure.'

'It's a beautiful box,' she said.

I managed to force open the box. I threw back the lid. We both looked in amazement. The box was empty!

'The treasure is lost,' said Miss Morstan calmly.

I listened to her words and suddenly realised what they meant: now there was no barrier between myself and Miss Morstan!

'Thank God!' I cried.

She looked at me.

'Why do you say that?' she asked.

'Because now I can tell you how I feel,' I said, taking her hand. 'I love you, Mary. The treasure stopped me from speaking. But now it has gone I can tell you I love you. That's why I said, "Thank God."'

She did not take her hand from mine. 'Then I say "Thank God" too,' she said.

One treasure was lost, but I had found another.

When I got to Baker Street, I showed them the empty box. Athelney Jones was very angry.

'You did this, Small,' he said.

'Yes, I did,' said Jonathan Small. 'It's my treasure and if I can't have it, then no one else can. No one has any right to it except three men who are in prison in the Andaman Islands and myself. It belongs to the sign of the four.'

'We have not heard your story,' said Holmes. 'We don't know if justice is on your side or not. Perhaps you can tell us.'

So Jonathan Small told us his side of the story.

'When I was eighteen, I joined the army and was sent to India. I went swimming in the Ganges. [1] A crocodile took my right leg, just above the knee. I was in hospital for five months and came out with this wooden leg. I was only twenty and I could no longer be in the army.

'But I found work on a plantation; [2] I was still able to ride a horse and I watched over the plantation and its workers for Mr

---

1. **the Ganges** : a sacred river in India.
2. **plantation** : large piece of land where tea, cotton, sugar, coffee etc. are grown.

Abel White. I was happy to spend the rest of my life there. But then came the Great Mutiny. [1] The plantation was burned and I had to escape. I went to Agra. There was a group of British people there. We moved into the old fort at Agra. The fort is an enormous building with many passages and doors. I guarded one of the doors with two other men, two Sikhs called Mahomet Singh and Abdullah Khan. One night, they suddenly took my gun and put a knife to my throat.

'"Listen to me," said one of them. "You are either with us, or you die. Do you understand?"

'I did not have much choice, so I agreed. Then they told me about the treasure. They said that it was to be divided four ways; among us three and another man called Dost Akbar. We made a promise to each other. Then they told me about a rich man who put his most valuable jewels in an iron box. He gave it to a servant to bring to the fort of Agra to be kept safe until the fighting was over.

'"The servant is disguised as a merchant and calls himself Achmet," they said. "He is in Agra now and is trying to find a way into the fort. Dost Akbar is with him and he is going to bring him to this door tonight. No one else knows he is coming, only us four. We will kill Achmet and divide the treasure between us."'

---

1. **the Great Mutiny** : a rebellion against the British in India (see dossier p. 82).

The text and **beyond**

1 **Comprehension check**

Choose the correct question word and answer the questions about Chapter Nine.

1   *Who/Why* killed Mr Sholto?

2   *Where/What* was the ship from Gravesend going?

3   *When/What* does Watson take to Miss Morstan?

4   *Why/Who* was Watson happy that there was no treasure?

5   *Who/When* took the treasure?

6   *When/What* did Mr Small escape to Agra?

7   *Why/Where* was Jonathan Small when he made the agreement?

8   *Why/Who* did they want to kill the servant?

2 **Picture summary**

Put the pictures in order and then write a short summary of Jonathan Small's story so far.

Example: *When he was ... he went to... A crocodile...*

'He says he knew nothing of the Norwood Murder'
→ He said that he knew nothing of the Norwood Murder

We often use **said** or **told** (+ person) in reported statements.

Usually the tense goes one step back.

'The treasure is very old,' he said.

→   He **said** (that) the treasure **was** very old.

or   He **told us** that the treasure **was** very old.

'We **told** him nothing,' he said.

→   He said (that) they **had told** him nothing.

When we make reported questions we do not invert the verb and subject and there is no question mark (?) at the end of the sentence.

'Where **is** the key?' asked Holmes.

→   Holmes **asked** Small where the key **was**.

'**Is** that the treasure?' she asked.

→   She **asked if** that **was** the treasure.

Remember: in reported speech other words (pronouns, adverbs, possessive adjectives, etc.) change

e.g. *my* → *his, today* → *that day, last week* → *the previous week*

3 **Reported speech**

Write a report of the interview with the suspect by completing the sentences in reported speech. Then practise the interview with a partner.

Athelney Jones: Is this the only boat you have, Mr Smith?

Mordecai Smith: I only have one boat, sir.

Athelney Jones: Where was the boat going?

Mordecai Smith: Gravesend.

Athelney Jones: Tell me once more, Mr Smith: what do you know about the treasure?

Mordecai Smith: I've already told you. I don't know anything about the treasure.

Athelney Jones: It is a crime to lie to a police officer, Mordecai Smith.

Mordecai Smith: I know nothing about the treasure, or the murder, I promise!

Report of interview with the suspect

1 I asked if ....
2 He replied that ....
3 I asked where ....
4 He said that ....
5 I wanted to confirm ....
6 He repeated that ....
7 I told him that ....
8 He promised that ....

FCE ❹ Crime doesn't pay

For questions 1-10, read the text below and decide which answer (A, B, C or D) best fits each space. There is an example at the beginning (0).

Police (**0**) ..A̱...... a 46 year old man in Las Vegas after they found (**1**) .... giving $100 dollar notes to people in the street from the money he had robbed from a (**2**) .... bank.

The man had gone into the bank with a gun. He gave a (**3**) .... to the cashier telling her to give him all the money in the safe.

Then he walked (**4**) .... out of the (**5**) .... and started (**6**) .... the money with (**7**) .... in the square in front of the bank.

One man, who was eating his lunch, asked him where he had (**8**) .... the money from and why he was giving him the money.

'I have (**9**) .... robbed a bank,' Mr Chroniak replied. 'Have (**10**) .... nice day!'

0 **A** arrested   **B** halted   **C** stopped   **D** accused
1 **A** her   **B** them   **C** him   **D** he
2 **A** close   **B** nearby   **C** near   **D** far
3 **A** letter   **B** sign   **C** note   **D** email
4 **A** coldly   **B** shyly   **C** angrily   **D** calmly
5 **A** building   **B** palace   **C** house   **D** hotel
6 **A** sharing   **B** dividing   **C** parting   **D** showing
7 **A** persons   **B** people   **C** person   **D** man
8 **A** received   **B** left   **C** got   **D** took
9 **A** just   **B** still   **C** yet   **D** never
10 **A** the   **B** a   **C** an   **D** some

5 Speaking

1 What do you think the saying 'crime doesn't pay' means? Choose an answer — A, B, or C. Talk about your choice in groups.

   A ☐ Being a criminal will only cause you problems in the end.

   B ☐ Most criminals lose the money they steal.

   C ☐ If the police catch you, you won't get any money in jail.

2 Do you agree that 'crime doesn't pay'?

FCE 6 Writing

You have seen a news story with the heading:

Criminals are not very clever.

Write a letter to the newspaper giving your opinions (120-180 words).

The Andaman Islands

One of the most interesting characters in *The Sign of Four* is Tonga, the little man from the Andaman Islands. Watson describes Tonga as a very small, dark-skinned man who uses poisoned darts he fires through a blowpipe. Jonathan Small describes the time when they made money by showing Tonga at fairs as 'the black cannibal'. How many of these descriptions are actually true? But first, let's find out more about the islands.

The Andaman Islands are an archipelago [1] of around two hundred tropical islands in the Bay of Bengal, quite a long way from India. The British used them as a penal colony [2] in 1858 during the time of the Indian Mutiny (see page 84).

The islands were too small on their own to qualify as a state of the newly independent Union of India in 1947, so the Andaman and the nearby Nicobar Islands were combined to make a Union Territory, a region with less political importance than a state. The two groups together make up about five hundred small islands. Approximately 350,000 people live on thirty or forty of these islands. Many of these are indigenous tribes. Among them are the Andaman Negritos, the Great Andamanese, the Onge, the Sentinelese and the Jarawas.

In today's world there are thousands of tribes who are near cultural and physical extinction. This is the case for the tribes who live on the Andaman Islands. They are among the most unusual people alive today. No other living human population has lived for so long in isolation from other groups of humans. Genetic evidence suggests

1. **archipelago** : a group of small islands.
2. **penal colony** : a place where prisoners are sent.

The Jarawas go fishing at the end of each day. The women use fishing nets but the men use bows and arrows.

that these people have existed for between 30,000 to 60,000 years. The way of life of these tribes is probably the most ancient in the world today.

It is true that the Andamanese are among the shortest people in the world. African pygmies are the world's other smallest tribe of people. It is also true that the colour of their skin is very dark. The different tribes on the Andaman islands are also different in their approach to strangers. Some tribes, such as the Onge, can be friendly and helpful. They have allowed scientists to study them in order to understand them better. But other tribes, such as the Sentinelese, resist any contact with the rest of the world. It is reported that they have used their blowpipes to attack people who have tried to approach them.

But there is no evidence at all that they are cannibals. When the Andamanese discovered that this is what the world thought of them, they were angry. The story has probably come from the fact that if strangers were killed on the islands they were burnt on the beaches. Some tribes hang their dead from branches of trees: this is to honour them by letting nature 'take them'. Europeans travellers probably imagined that this was like the European way of hanging their criminals. The islanders also sometimes wear bones and skulls as part of their dress. If people from ships at sea saw this, then they might assume that the islanders had actually eaten their dead.

Sadly, the numbers of these tribes are diminishing. At the beginning of the twentieth century, there were 677 people belonging to the Onge tribe. In 1991, there were only 101. Newcomers and tourists have populated the islands and have brought diseases with them. Because these tribes have lived in isolation from the rest of humanity for so long, they have little or no immunity to modern diseases.

The Andamanese are Indian citizens, even if they do not know it. In the troubled time of independence in 1947 (see page 84) the Andaman islands were not a priority issue. So, a new governor was appointed for the Islands every few years. Until 2004, these governors were usually military men or older officials from the main government who were going to retire soon, who were not completely committed to doing what was right for the islanders.

But then the tsunami of 26 December 2004 occurred. The islands were so close to the epicentre of the Asian earthquake that the tsunami hit them almost immediately. The effects of the tsunami were dealt with inefficiently, and this showed that the islands were governed poorly. Interestingly, the indigenous population of the Andaman islands were not affected by the tsunami in the same way as the Indian population because they knew when to stay away from

Many of the **Andaman and Nicobar islands** are still wild, but they are gradually becoming a tourist destination.

the sea, and after feeling the earthquake they followed their instincts and went to the higher ground.

Some people believe that it is better to leave these tribes to live as they have for so long a time: Indian civilisation will survive without the Andamanese, but the Andamanese will not survive if they are brought into Indian civilisation.

1 **Comprehension check**

Answer the questions about the Andaman Islands.

1　Where are the Andaman Islands?
2　How many islands are there in the archipelago?
3　Which country governs the region?
4　Which other group of islands is part of the state?
5　Why were the islands badly governed?
6　What happened in 2004?

Comprehension check

Tick the facts about the indigenous Andamanese that are true. Correct the false ones with the correct information.

1. ☐ The Andamanese are among the most ancient tribes in the world.
2. ☐ There are five main tribes.
3. ☐ They are no smaller than most people from South Asia.
4. ☐ They can be hostile to outsiders.
5. ☐ They are cannibals.
6. ☐ They are fully integrated into Indian culture.

 INTERNET PROJECT

Connect to the Internet and go to www.blackcat-cideb.com or www.cideb.it. Insert the title or part of the title of the book into our search engine. Open the page for *The Sign of Four*. Click on the Internet project link.

Find out more about the Andaman Islands.

How can you get to the islands?

What can you do there?

What can you find out about local festivals and events?

Before you read

1 **What do you think?**

Discuss this question with another student.

How do you think Jonathan Small's story will end?

Example: I *think the four men will kill the servant and then hide the treasure in...*

CHAPTER **TEN**

The Story of the Wooden-Legged Man

Jonathan Small continued his story.

'I was surrounded by death and killing every day, so the death of Achmet didn't mean much to me. I promised the two other men that I was with them.

'Achmet and Dost Akbar arrived. The three Sikhs took Achmet away with them. I heard a fight and then Achmet escaped; he came running back past me with the others chasing him. I put out my foot to make him fall and Dost Akbar killed him.'

Jonathan Small stopped for a moment. We all looked disgusted.

'Well, if you were in my place, you might have done the same,' he said defiantly. [1]

'Go on with the story,' said Holmes.

---

1. **defiantly** : aggressively and obstinately.

'We buried the body and then opened the box with the treasure inside. There were a lot of beautiful gems inside: diamonds, rubies, emeralds, pearls. We counted them all and then put them back in the box. We decided to hide the box until we could leave the fort safely. I drew four maps, one for each of us, to show where the treasure was. I put the sign of the four at the bottom. We promised that each of us should act for all four of us, never just for himself.

'Soon, it seemed that peace was coming once again to India and we hoped that soon we could share the treasure and escape safely. But we were arrested for the murder of Achmet. We were put in prison for life. The treasure stayed where it was.

'We were moved to the Andaman Islands. I was treated very well there. All the time I was thinking of ways to escape and return to Agra but I was hundreds of miles away from any other land. It was difficult.

'Often, I watched the soldiers and the prison officers playing cards in the evenings. There was Major Sholto, Captain Morstan and some others. The soldiers always lost. Major Sholto was the worst. Soon he had lost all his money and was drinking a lot.

'I saw my chance. One night I asked him what was the right thing to do with the hidden treasure. I told him it was worth half a million. His eyes lit up. He spoke to Captain Morstan. He said that perhaps they could help. We made a deal: they helped me and my three friends to freedom, and they got a fifth share of the treasure. Major Sholto didn't think this was much although it was fifty thousand for each of them.

'We had a second meeting with Mahomet Singh, Abdullah Khan and Dost Akbar. We came to an agreement: I made them

two maps of the fort to show where the treasure was hidden. Major Sholto would go to Agra to check that the box was there. He would leave it there and arrange for a small boat to come to the islands for me and my three friends. We would then go to Agra in the boat and Major Sholto would return to the island. Then Captain Morstan would meet us in Agra and then divide the treasure. Captain Morstan would take the major's share to him. The sign of the four was on each map. We waited.

'Major Sholto went to India but never came back. We found out that his uncle had died and left him a lot of money. He had also taken our treasure. Captain Morstan went to Agra but it was gone. From then on I thought only of revenge. It became more important than the treasure itself.

'Some time after, I helped one of the Andaman Islanders when he was ill. When he was better, he wanted to stay with me. I learned to speak a little of his language. Tonga (that was his name) had a large canoe. He helped me to escape from the island. We travelled around the world for a while, my small friend and I. Eventually we arrived in England. I found out where Sholto lived and I soon found out that he still had the jewels.

'When I heard that he was dying, I went over to the house. I saw him with his two sons, but I knew I was too late. He was already dead. I went back later to search for some clue about the treasure but there was nothing. I left the note saying "The sign of the four".

'We made some money at this time by showing Tonga at fairs and circuses: "The world's smallest man" or "The Cannibal". We made enough to live and eat. Then I heard that the sons had found the treasure. I knew that with Tonga's help we could get it.

Unfortunately, Bartholomew Sholto was still in the room when we went to get the treasure. Tonga thought he had done something very clever by killing him so he was very surprised when I was so angry. And the rest of the story, you already know.'

'A remarkable [1] story,' said Holmes.

'I think it's time to take our story-teller away,' said Athelney Jones. 'The cab is waiting. Thank you both for your help. Good night.'

'Good night, gentlemen,' said Jonathan Small.

We sat smoking in silence for a while after they left.

'I'm afraid that may be the last investigation I can help with, Holmes.' I said finally. 'Miss Morstan has accepted my offer of marriage.'

Sherlock Holmes groaned. [2]

'What's wrong?' I asked.

'Nothing,' he said. 'She is a charming young lady. But love is an emotional thing and emotion is the opposite of reason, which I value above everything else.'

Holmes looked tired.

'It seems rather unfair,' I said, 'you have done all the work in this business. I get a wife out of it, Jones takes all the credit and what do you get?'

'For me,' said Sherlock Holmes, 'there is always the next case.'

---

1. **remarkable** : unusual and interesting.
2. **groaned** : made a sound expressing disapproval.

The text and **beyond**

FCE ❶ **Comprehension check**

For questions 1-7 choose the answer — A, B, C or D — which you think fits best according to the text.

1 Who killed the servant?
- A ☐ Jonathan Small
- B ☐ Dost Akbar
- C ☐ They all did.
- D ☐ He fell by accident.

2 What did they do with the treasure chest?
- A ☐ They took it with them.
- B ☐ They buried it with the body.
- C ☐ They hid it in the fort.
- D ☐ They took it to the Andaman Islands.

3 Why did Jonathan Small know Major Sholto would be interested?
- A ☐ He had lost all his money through playing cards.
- B ☐ He was drinking heavily.
- C ☐ He and Captain Morstan wanted to go to Agra.
- D ☐ It was a lot of money for a greedy man like him.

4 What was the plan for Captain Morstan?
- A ☐ Go to Agra after Major Sholto had organised a boat for him.
- B ☐ Divide the treasure and take back Major Sholto's share.
- C ☐ Take the treasure and return to the island.
- D ☐ Take the treasure and tell Major Sholto so he could rescue them.

5 How did Jonathan Small meet his friend?
- A ☐ He met him at a travelling circus.
- B ☐ He was the servant of the prison officers.
- C ☐ He helped him on the island when he was ill.
- D ☐ He used his boat to escape from the island.

6   What happened to Jonathan Small after he told his story.

   A ☐ He went to get back the treasure.

   B ☐ He got into a cab with them.

   C ☐ He was free to go.

   D ☐ The police took him to prison.

7   What does Sherlock Holmes think of Watson's marriage to Miss Morstan?

   A ☐ That she is a charming young lady and he is lucky.

   B ☐ That she is too rich for Watson.

   C ☐ That he has done the wrong thing.

   D ☐ That love is too emotional for someone like Holmes.

2 Characters

Can you remember who said these things in the story? Write their names and match them to their reason for saying it (A-F).

1   E 'I hate to be bored.'   Sherlock Holmes

2   ☐ 'I have treated Morstan's daughter terribly.'   ....

3   ☐ 'My brother is very like my father, …'   ....

4   ☐ 'Well, I say 'Thank God!' too.'   ....

5   ☐ 'You might have done the same.'   ....

6   ☐ 'I'm afraid that may be the last investigation I can help with.'   ....

A   She was happy Watson would ask her to marry him.

B   He was going to marry Miss Morstan.

C   He wanted them to believe he did it because his life was at risk.

D   He had not told her about her father's share of the treasure.

E   He wanted a new case to investigate.

F   He was greedy and did not want to give Miss Morstan the treasure.

3 What do you think?

Choose the answer closest to your opinion. Then discuss the
questions with another student, giving some opinions of your own.

1 Can Holmes really know everything from his observations?
   A ☐ Yes, he is a very clever and logical man.
   B ☐ No, he knows a lot of people who give him some of this
         information.
   C ☐ No, some of it he is able to deduce correctly, the rest is luck.

2 Do you think Jonathan Small should go to prison?
   A ☐ Yes, he helped murder a man and steal treasure that was
         not his.
   B ☐ Yes, but not for long. He is not a bad man, just a bit greedy.
   C ☐ No, he did not kill anyone and he wanted justice for his
         friends, too.

3 Will Sherlock Holmes ever get married?
   A ☐ Yes, when he meets the right person.
   B ☐ No, he loves his work too much.
   C ☐ No. Even if he is in love, he will find a reason not to marry.

4 Consequences – writing a funny mystery story

Work in pairs. Student A writes a name at the top of a piece of paper
(1) and folds it so Student B can't see. Student B writes the word
'murdered' + a name (2) and folds the paper again. In turns make a
short story.

Student A write:

- (3) The place where this person murdered the other.
- (5) Write 'he/she said to the police' + what he/she said.
- (7) What this person did after they spoke to the police.

Student B write:

- (4) How this person was killed.
- (6) Write 'the police said' + what they said.
- (8) What happened to the criminal at the end (the consequence).

5 **Writing**

Now write your own short mystery story in about 200 words.
Begin with the line:

It all happened on a cold winter's night...

Remember to include:

- Who killed who?
- How they killed the victim.
- What was the consequence?

....
....
....
....
....
....
....
....
....
....
....

6 **Word puzzle**

Find the solutions to the questions and complete the word puzzle.

1 At the end of the story, only Jonathan Small knew where the .... was.

2 A woman who inherits a lot of money.

3 This helps you to solve a crime.

4   Holmes lives in Baker ....

5   Watson didn't want Miss Morstan to .... a lot of money.

6   Jonathan Small came to look for Major Sholto when the major was ....

7   Jonathan Small met Captain Morstan and Major Sholto in these islands.

8   Miss Morstan received a pearl every year, which she kept in a small ....

9   Miss Morstan worked for Mrs Cecil ....

10   The name of Jonathan Small's small friend.

11   Thaddeus Sholto wanted to give Miss Morstan .... of the treasure.

12   Holmes says that knowledge comes with ....

13   Holmes finds some very small .... at the scene of the crime.

14   Holmes deduced things from what he ....

15   When something or someone is strange or not ordinary.

16   A bad thing done by another person can make you want this.

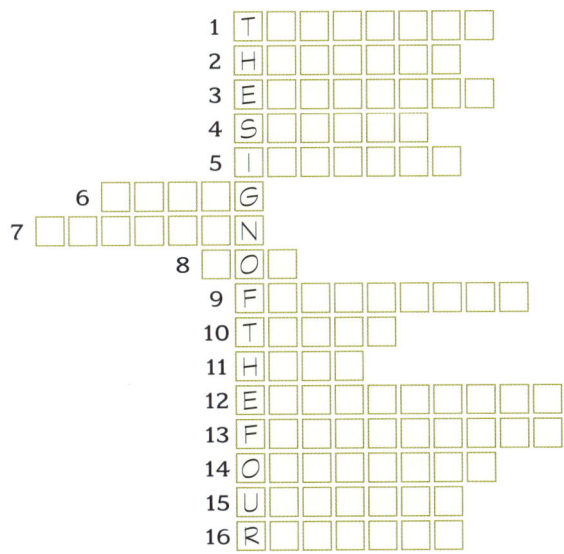

7 Picture Summary

Look at these pictures from the story. Which chapters do they come from? Put them in the correct order and describe what is happening in each scene.

1 Comprehension check

Answer these questions about the story.

1. What is Sherlock Holmes able to deduce in Chapter One?
2. Why did Miss Morstan want to meet the man outside the Lyceum theatre?
3. How did Captain Morstan die?
4. Who lived at Pondicherry House?
5. How did Holmes know the man with a wooden leg was Jonathan Small?
6. Where did Toby take Holmes and Watson?
7. Who were the 'Baker Street Boys'?
8. Who helped Jonathan Small and Tonga?
9. Why did the 'Sign of Four' kill the servant?
10. Did the police and Holmes find the treasure in the end?

2 The case

Describe the case Miss Mary Morstan asks Sherlock Holmes to investigate.

Example: Miss Mary Morstan had received a note...

....
....
....
....

3 The plot

Put these events from chapters 3-8 in order.

A ☐ Holmes speaks to the woman at the boatyard.

B ☐ The two men escape in the *Aurora*, followed by the police.

C ☐ Watson goes to Miss Morstan and Mrs Forrester to tell them about the discovery at the boatyard.

D ☐ Holmes dresses as a sailor to find out where the men have gone.

E ☐ They hear the story about how Captain Morstan died.

F ☐ Bartholomew Sholto is found dead in his room and the treasure is gone.

G ☐ A man takes them to the house of Major Sholto's son.

H ☐ Tonga falls in the river and then Jonathan Small gets stuck at the side of the river.

I ☐ Holmes and Watson investigate the case at Pondicherry House.

J ☐ Holmes and Watson discover the identity of the man with the small footprints.

FCE ❹ **Summary**

Complete this summary of Jonathan Small's story from Chapters Nine and Ten. There is an example at the beginning (0).

Jonathan Small joined the army and was (0) ..B̲..... to India. In India a crocodile bit his leg off and he was given a wooden leg. Because he was unfit for service, he found (1) .... on a plantation. He was very happy on the plantation but there was a big rebellion and the plantation was burned, (2) .... he had to escape.

He went to the city of Agra. There he guarded the fort with two (3) .... men. One night they told him of their plan to kill a servant who was going to hide the jewels of his rich master in the fort until the (4) .... was over.

They killed the servant and hid the treasure in the fort. Jonathan Small made a map for them all and they (5) .... a promise to always act together.

They were arrested for the murder of Achmet and sent to the Andaman Islands. In prison Jonathan Small spoke to one of the prison (6) ...., Major Sholto and persuaded him to go and look for the treasure in return for a share with another soldier, Captain Morstan. He would (7) .... the treasure to them and help them escape.

In the end Major Sholto went to Agra and disappeared with the treasure. Finally Jonathan Small was able to escape (8) .... the Islands with the help of an islander (9) .... he had looked after when he was ill. He went to England and earned money by showing his new friend, Tonga, in the circus. But Jonathan Small wanted to find the treasure and (10) .... his revenge.

0	**A** went	Ⓑ sent	**C** took	**D** gone
1	**A** work	**B** job	**C** worked	**D** employed
2	**A** that	**B** because	**C** however	**D** so
3	**A** and	**B** other	**C** extra	**D** India

4	**A** fighting	**B** fights	**C** fought	**D** fighter
5	**A** did	**B** had	**C** made	**D** was
6	**A** soldier	**B** captain	**C** guards	**D** person
7	**A** bring	**B** took	**C** hold	**D** have
8	**A** away	**B** from	**C** of	**D** to
9	**A** who	**B** which	**C** when	**D** where
10	**A** want	**B** had	**C** took	**D** get

5 The conclusion

How does the story end? Choose an answer — A, B, C or D.

A ☐ Watson marries and Holmes has a new case.

B ☐ Watson is going to marry but Holmes is only interested in the next case.

C ☐ Athelney Jones arrests Jonathan Small and Holmes receives his payment.

D ☐ Holmes and Watson discuss the case.

6 Themes

Choose four words from the box that you think best describe the themes in this story.

> greed   passion   revenge   war   religion   friendship
> violence   justice   children

Answers to the crime quiz (p. 61): 1 A; 2 A; 3 C; 4 B; 5 B; 6 C.

Key to Exit Test

1 1 He is able to deduce that Watson went to the post office and sent a telegram that morning, and also that Watson's watch had belonged to Watson's father and then his brother. 2 Because she wants to find out what happened to her father. 3 He had a heart attack, fell and hit his head. 4 Major John Sholto and his sons. 5 Because Major Sholto had shot at a white wooden-legged man and Jonathan Small was the only white man of the four men. 6 He took them to the edge of the river. 7 Homeless children who lived on the streets and who sometimes work for Holmes. 8 Mordecai Smith. 9 Because he had the treasure and if they killed him no one would know where the treasure was. 10 No, they didn't.

2 Open answer.

3 A 6; B 9; C 7; D 8; E 2; F 3; G 1; H 10; I 4; J 5;

4 1 A; 2 D; 3 B; 4 A; 5 C; 6 C; 7 A; 8 B; 9 A; 10 D

5 B

6 greed justice revenge friendship (passion and violence are also possible but this is not shown very strongly).

This reader uses the **EXPANSIVE READING** approach, where the text becomes a springboard to improve language skills and to explore historical background, cultural connections and other topics suggested by the text.

The new structures introduced in this step of our **READING & TRAINING** series are listed below. Naturally, structures from lower steps are included too. For a complete list of structures used over all the six steps, see *The Black Cat Guide to Graded Readers*, which is also downloadable at no cost from our website, www.blackcat-cideb.com or www.cideb.it.

The vocabulary used at each step is carefully checked against vocabulary lists used for internationally recognised examinations.

Step **Four** B2.1

All the structures used in the previous levels, plus the following:

Verb tenses
Present Perfect Simple: *the first / second* etc. *time that ...*
Present Perfect Continuous: unfinished past with *for* or *since* (duration form)

Verb forms and patterns
Passive forms: Present Perfect Simple
Reported speech introduced by precise reporting verbs (e.g. *suggest, promise, apologise*)

Modal verbs
Be / get used to + -ing: habit formation
Had better: duty and warning

Types of clause
3rd Conditional: *if* + Past Perfect, *would(n't) have*
Conditionals with *may / might*
Non-defining relative clauses with: *which, whose*
Clauses of concession: *even though*; *in spite of*, *despite*

Step Four B2.1